DELAYED DEPARTURE

This is a truly important book containing some valuable information and in-depth evaluation of soul rescue. An often misunderstood subject, but in this case it is clarified and explained in a really lucid manner and can help all those who are interested in finding out more about this important subject.

Tony Neate, co-founder of College of Healing, past chair of Spirit Release Foundation, founder of Nature's Own/Cytoplan Nutrition Group, counselor/healer/channeler, and author of *Channelling for Everyone*, 1997, now in its 6th reprint

Delayed Departure

A Beginner's Guide to Soul Rescue

Delayed Departure

A Beginner's Guide to Soul Rescue

Ann Merivale

Illustrations by Karen Roberts

BOOKS

Winchester, UK
Washington, USA

First published by Sixth Books, 2013
Sixth Books is an imprint of John Hunt Publishing Ltd., Laurel House, Station Approach,
Alresford, Hants, SO24 9JH, UK
office1@jhpbooks.net
www.johnhuntpublishing.com
www.6th-books.com

For distributor details and how to order please visit the 'Ordering' section on our website.

Text copyright: Ann Merivale 2013

ISBN: 978 1 78279 011 2

A CIP catalogue record for this book is available from the British Library.

Design: Stuart Davies

Cover design by Rowan Taliesin www.rowantaliesin.com

Printed and bound by CPI Group (UK) Ltd, Croydon, CR0 4YY

We operate a distinctive and ethical publishing philosophy in all
areas of our business, from our global network of authors to
production and worldwide distribution.

CONTENTS

For Dr. Roger Woolger, my mentor, the well-known Jungian psychoanalyst, esteemed author of books on past-life regression, and the founder of Deep Memory Process therapy. He died on 18 November 2011, exactly one month before his sixty-seventh birthday, and is now sorely missed by many people worldwide. Without his influence I would certainly not have got involved in soul rescue. I know for sure that he will be continuing on the other side with his important work and look forward to rejoining him in it once my own work here is complete.

Acknowledgements

For this book I am indebted firstly to Simon Buxton, without whose Sacred Trust workshop on 'Death, Dying and the Beyond' it would never have happened. Lawrence does an excellent job of keeping me at it when I so easily get distracted by other things in life, and for some of the content I am grateful both to him and to the 'Mouliners' group (a branch of the Woolger crowd!) for comments and advice. And of that precious group I particularly thank Lynn Dunne for suggesting the perfect main title when that was eluding me.

My husband David has proved himself, as always, invaluable for minor points of editing, and has on occasion helped me to find the right word when that also was eluding me.

I owe a huge thank-you to my good friends Rowan Taliesin for the cover design and Karen Roberts for the illustrations, and of course to John Hunt, Barbara Ford Hammond and all those at 6th Books for their cooperation and efficiency.

Last but by no means least, I am grateful to Ananda, my spirit guide, both for this particular book and for my soul rescue work, and to Sathya Sai Baba, the avatar of our age, who oversees all the most important aspects of my life.

I

Introduction

Be careful, then, be gentle about death.
For it is hard to die, it is difficult to go through
the door, even when it opens.

And the poor dead, when they have left the walled
and silvery city of the now hopeless body,
where are they to go? Oh, where are they to go?
D. H. Lawrence, 'All Souls' Day'

In M. Night Shyamalan's film/movie *The Sixth Sense*, Bruce Willis played the part of Dr. Malcolm Crowe, a distinguished child psychologist who is shot by a former client (now grown up) whom he had failed to help. The fact that one cannot help everyone is often a difficult, but important, lesson for therapists to learn. In Malcolm's case the awareness of having 'failed' in just one case rendered him unable to cross over straight away; he remained for a while 'trapped' on the Earth's plane. Furthermore, dying so suddenly made it impossible for him to say his 'goodbyes' to his beloved wife, and his subsequent efforts to communicate with her led only to frustration and feelings of rejection.

This story is of course fictional, but it nevertheless conveys a good deal of truth, since failure to cross over immediately after death is in fact a much more common problem than most of us appreciate. Everyone has heard, for instance, of 'black spots', where repeated road accidents occur, but how many people understand the reason why they are there? Well, they are caused by the presence of the 'ghost' of an accident victim who died too quickly to be aware of what had happened and is therefore stuck in the spot. Such souls are unable to cross over to the other side simply because they do not realize that they are dead, and their presence, combined with the memory of what happened to them that is printed in the ether, troubles other drivers and consequently perpetuates the tendency towards further accidents occurring at the spot concerned. Wars in the world are perpetuated partly by souls whose own battle is long since over, but who know nothing else; and houses can be haunted by their previous owners who are unwilling to pass their dwellings on to others.

One might well wonder – as I used to – why such 'ghosts' cannot be helped to cross over by some of the many advanced souls on the other side who are aware of their predicament. The answer seems to be that, although there are indeed numerous spirit helpers whose job it is to help and advise the lost ones, they cannot initially get through to people who are trapped in what is all they currently know (or remember), namely, the physical world. For that reason, for the post-physical death transition to be made, assistance is often required from someone who is still on Earth in a physical body. People who are confused (as Malcolm was after being killed so very suddenly), or totally unaware that they no longer have a physical body, will much more easily communicate with someone who is still on Earth whom they can easily see – someone to whom they feel they can relate.

The movie character Malcolm was painfully conscious of having 'failed' one of the children he had treated in the past, and the solution he found to his dilemma was promptly to latch on to Cole, a young boy who was badly needing psychological help following his parents' divorce. The loss of his father was, however, not Cole's only problem; he was also extremely psychic and was constantly plagued by lost souls who were asking for help. Although the case in the film may have been somewhat exaggerated, there is no doubt that the ability to see 'dead' people as clearly as live ones is, if fairly unusual, by no means unique.

The fact that Cole could see 'Dr. Crowe' so clearly, and responded slowly but surely to his attempts to treat him in the way that he had treated other children while he was alive, must have delayed Malcolm's full realization that he had been killed. (He attributed his grieving wife's failure to respond to him to a change of character on his own part.)

Dr. Crowe's and Cole's story had a happy ending: receiving treatment from a deceased psychologist, who *believed* the fact that he saw dead people, eventually enabled the boy to reveal his secret to his mother and thus improve their relationship. And Malcolm firstly took the boy's advice to talk to his wife while she was asleep, and secondly 'redeemed himself' in his own eyes by helping Cole. Once he had told his wife how much he loved her, and completed Cole's treatment, he felt able to move on from the Earth's plane. But many lost souls are alas not able to resolve their issues on their own and then make a transition, and these are the ones that are so greatly needing our help.

Shamanism has for long understood this and, in the areas of Africa where the Churches have not completely stamped out traditional religion, the newly deceased are helped by their survivors to cross over. But modern science, with its constant demand for visible physical proof of everything, does little to encourage understanding of what tends to be known as the 'paranormal'. Michael Harner says in his classic book *The Way of the Shaman*[1] that both archaeological and ethnological evidence suggests that shamanic healing methods are *at least* 20,000–30,000 years old, and that the practices which have been handed down over the centuries are very similar in completely different parts of the globe. The word *shaman*, which is possibly a Russian one (though there appears to be no consensus as to its origin), means something akin to a 'communicator between the human and spirit worlds'. Jeremy Naydler[2] aptly describes the role of the shaman as 'mediator between the "nonordinary reality" of the spirit world and the ordinary reality of the sense perceptible world'.

So, if you are willing to spend, for instance, just an hour a week helping these stuck souls to cross over and thus contribute to clearing our world's polluted atmosphere, I hope that this book will be a good starting point for you. However, I should initially point out that when I myself first embarked on soul rescue work, I had already done a great deal of training and practice in Deep Memory Process therapy (otherwise known as past-life regression). It was probably at least partly thanks to this that soul rescue work came to me more quickly and easily than I had expected. Consequently, to anyone for whom the concepts of shamanism and communication with spirits are new, I strongly recommend that you first do a little reading – and preferably also attend at least one shamanic workshop – before proceeding further with the work on which I am about to elaborate. Once you have familiarized yourself with a few basic concepts, I am sure that this fascinating and rewarding work could come at least as easily to you, the reader, as it did to me.

The Michael Harner book I have just mentioned is a good introduction, and I also strongly recommend *Shamanism: The Book of Journeys* by Robert Levy and Dr. Eve Bruce[3] as well as the latter's earlier book.[4] For workshops, I can recommend The Sacred Trust[5] from personal experience, but I know that there are many other excellent teachers around. Good names to look for in Britain are John and Caitlin Matthews or Duncan Wordley, and Dr. Eve Bruce is now living and working in Ireland, where she offers workshops jointly with her partner Michael Travers (see www.dolphinspiritgate.com). Alberto Villoldo's 'Four Winds' training is also highly reputed, and he teaches in numerous different places and has also written several books.[6]

We are now well into 2012 and racing at breakneck speed towards the celebrated Mayan date of 21 December. What exactly will happen on that day – or indeed how precise the date is, since the Mayan calendars were so different from our Gregorian one –

is at the time of writing as yet unclear, but no one can deny either the fact that the world is currently in turmoil, or that time is speeding up. This means that any assistance with cleaning things up cannot come too quickly.

If you are already involved in a Green movement of some sort, or even simply thinking about how to live yourself in a more ecologically friendly way, then so much the better, but that is not the subject of this book. There are already many books around that tackle these issues excellently. My concern here, as you will by now have gathered, is cleaning up our precious Earth's 'invisible' realms, and that of course does not involve putting pressure on intransigent governments.

The solution is simple, and if enough people join forces to work on it, we will be able not only to bring about a 'cleaner' world, but also to release many lost souls who have been suffering for what may well have been centuries. No special skill or qualification is needed – simply commitment and a loving heart – and a brief period of practice will make perfect. My own experience of working as a Deep Memory Process (or past-life regression) therapist is useful, but by no means essential, and I rejoice in the thought that I shall still be able to perform soul rescue work even when I have become too decrepit to write any more books or continue with my therapy practice. So, whatever your age, qualifications or experience, please believe that you can be of real use and take my words seriously. If your answer to my plea is 'No, because I'm afraid it would involve too much hard work', and I then told you that you could do it flat on your back at home, would that make you more inclined to say 'Yes'? If so, please read on.

II

How This Book Came About

... which has been given as His promise, that God hath not willed that any soul should perish but hath with every temptation, every trial, every disappointment made a way of escape or for correcting same. It is not a way of justification only, as by faith, but a way to know, to realize that in these disappointments, separations, there comes the assurance that He cares!
Edgar Cayce, Reading 1567-2

For me, as a young Catholic in the 1940s to 1960s, things were supposedly fairly simple and straightforward. So long as you had been baptized, if you lived your one and only life on Earth reasonably well, committing not more than the average number of 'venial' sins, you could expect when you died to go initially to Purgatory. The images of Purgatory that were conveyed by the clergy or other teachers of 'the Faith' were fairly vague, but the general idea was that it was not a particularly pleasant place (or rather 'state' since places were said to exist only on Earth), and that the souls who were there were filled with yearning to see Jesus and God and to spend the rest of eternity in their company in Heaven. Only certain very exceptional people – the Mother Teresas or (possibly, since after all he was not a Christian!) the Gandhis of this world – could hope to bypass Purgatory and go straight to Heaven. How many days, week, months or years one was likely to spend in Purgatory was purely a matter for wild speculation, but one thing that was certain was that the period of the sentence could be reduced if one's family or friends had Masses said and prayed for the repose of one's soul. If, on the other hand, one committed any 'mortal' sins – for instance murder, adultery or deliberately missing Mass on a Sunday –

6

rather than being given the opportunity of 'purging' oneself in preparation for Heaven, one would, if one failed to repent on one's deathbed, be condemned to Hell for all eternity.

But the picture for those not fortunate enough to have been born into a Christian family was not quite as grim as the first phrase of my second sentence might suggest, because having water poured over one's head by a priest was not the only way to achieve baptism. Firstly, if a baby was dying and no priest was available, *anyone* could perform the ritual satisfactorily; and secondly there were two other possible forms of baptism: 'baptism by blood' and 'baptism by desire'. If you had not been exposed to Christianity but led a good life and were killed for what you believed in, then shedding your blood worked as well as did the sacrament with water. Or alternatively, if you had had the misfortune of having been brought up in some other religion, or as a 'heathen', but nevertheless acted as though you believed in Jesus and the one true God, *even if* you failed to acknowledge either, then you were deemed to have obtained 'baptism by desire'. (Gandhi would obviously have fallen into both these categories!) Things were slightly less good, however, for the poor babies who died where no water, or no person to administer the sacrament, was available. Since they had no passport to Heaven but had not lived long enough to commit either the venial sins that led to Purgatory or the mortal sins that condemned one to Hell, they were consigned to Limbo – a place that was not at all unpleasant, but which sounded as though it might become rather boring long before eternity was spent. (One thing for which I will credit Pope Benedict XVI is his statement that belief in Limbo is not mandatory, but that still leaves the Church in a dilemma, since the sacrament of baptism is considered to be essential for salvation.)

Were things, however, *really* so simple and straightforward? Well, they certainly weren't for me at any rate! When, at the age of between 7 and 8, I was being prepared for my First Holy

Communion at the Convent of Mercy in Bristol, England, by the good Mother Campion (named after the Blessed Edmund, whose sanctity had not yet been fully recognized, but who was surely well on the way to it!), I did not have the courage to question out loud what was being taught me. Yet I was constantly perplexed in my mind by paradoxes such as: 'If it's really true that God is all good and loves us all equally, how could He be so cruel as to condemn anyone to Hell for ever?' As I grew older, I was further tormented by other conflicts. On the one hand was the question: 'Why am I so unlucky as to have a father who can't stand the sight of me because I'm so ugly and terrible, while other children's parents think that they're wonderful and love them?' On the other hand, since I was *obviously* so unworthy, was the even greater perplexity: 'Why do I always have enough to eat and a nice house to live in while others have to live in hovels and starvation?' Yet I had to wait until I was approaching the age of 52 for some of these mysteries to begin to be solved for me!

In my first book[1] I recounted how a lecture on Edgar Cayce, the great American Christian seer, converted me to belief in reincarnation and karma, thus solving the dilemma of how God could be totally just; and in my second book[2] I wrote a bit about Cayce and also recommended books on him written by American authors. One thing led to another until, by the age of 58, I held a Diploma in Past-Life Regression Therapy and was practicing as a past-life regression therapist, undergoing further training in Deep Memory Process with Dr. Roger Woolger and writing more books on spiritual topics. As those years passed, firstly I devoured more and more illuminating books on the subject of the afterlife, marveling ever more and more at the ignorance of a Church which claims that the 'hereafter' is its main concern; and secondly the links between Dr. Woolger's work and shamanism became steadily stronger.

In July 2003, two and a quarter years after I had obtained my Woolger diploma, I attended an introductory 'Way of the

Shaman' weekend with Simon Buxton[3] of the Sacred Trust, who had trained with the distinguished American shaman, Michael Harner. I enjoyed that workshop so much that when, the following year, I saw that the Sacred Trust were putting on a weekend with Simon Buxton entitled 'Death, Dying and the Beyond', I registered for it immediately. (At that time I had the idea that I was going to be working with the dying at a later stage in my life. It was later that I realized that I was in fact going to be working with the dead rather than the dying!)

At this point I need to explain further why 'soul rescue' work is so very necessary. Other books have been written about the realms beyond the Earth's plane, and of them I should like to recommend particularly *A Soul's Journey* by Peter Richelieu[4] and *Destiny of Souls* by Dr. Michael Newton.[5] Also, my own book, *Discovering the Life Plan: Eleven Steps to Your Destiny*,[6] elaborates both on the 'descent' made prior to incarnating and on the 'ascent' that souls gradually make after death. So the only thing that needs to be mentioned here is the fact that the 'lowest' of these higher realms – the one immediately 'above' (for want of a better word) the Earth's plane and commonly known as the 'astral realms' – is, though etheric rather than physical, an exact replica of Earth. Consequently, unless someone has been adequately prepared for death, it is all too easy for them to fail to realize that they have left their physical body. And these 'ghosts' – particularly in the West, where education in these matters has been sadly lacking for hundreds of years – pollute, as I have stated, our atmosphere as well as inflicting on themselves an unnecessarily long Purgatory. (Yes, dear Roman Catholic Church, you are right in one way because both Purgatory and Hell do exist, but they are of our own making, not God's, and neither lasts for ever.)

Before I attended Simon Buxton's workshops, I was aware both from my reading and from my education in Woolger workshops that one of the tasks of a shaman was to travel to find lost souls who were stuck in the astral realms and to help them to cross over to the other side. In her first, and best-known, book, *Winged Pharaoh*,[7] which is about her previous life as the young Egyptian girl Sekeeta, Joan Grant's teacher explains to her on her return from the journeying that she did during her initiation, the predicament of an Earthbound male soul:

> People of his country know not what death is. They think that when their nostrils no longer draw breath, they shall have reached the end of consciousness. So, finding themselves still living, they think it must be upon Earth that they live. And in so thinking, they are bound by the limitations of Earth, from which they should be free... But he will listen, though it may take time.

What I was *not* prepared for at all was what spirit was asking of me from my attendance in London that weekend in November 2004.

But before I continue with my own story, I should like to mention something that this book is *not* dealing with. Getting stuck in the astral realms without a physical body is not the only possible scenario for a soul who has got lost. Many, for varying reasons, attach themselves to someone on Earth (very often a relative). The work of 'spirit releasement' was pioneered in the United States by the Baldwins,[8] Britain has a Spirit Release Foundation, people who train as regression therapists are normally expected to qualify in spirit releasement as well, and Roger Woolger latterly spent almost as much of his time doing 'ancestral healing' work as he did training people in Deep Memory Process therapy. When a therapist is performing a regression, the way she can elucidate whether she is dealing with a client's own past life or that of a spirit attachment is by finding out if the character who is speaking through the client knows that he or she is dead. But the release of spirits who are attached to someone living is not the subject of this book; you can turn elsewhere for that.

So, on the Saturday morning of that November weekend in 2004, after some initial explanation of the rescue work in which he was intending to involve the participants in his 'Death, Dying and the Beyond' workshop, Simon Buxton lost little time in plunging us in. He – as is necessary for someone in his profession – is a wonderful drummer, and his drum soon led a boatload of us all along a river to look for the power animals who were going to be assisting us in the search for souls needing help. (This exercise is known as 'psychopomp'.) Then, in the afternoon, each armed with our respective animal helpers, we embarked upon our first rescue mission. I had for many years bemoaned both my lack of clairvoyant ability and the fact that, unlike certain other people I knew, I never received messages from spirit. It is therefore difficult to describe my astonishment when, on that very first shamanic soul rescue journey that I made, I clearly heard a voice in my head saying, 'You're to do this psychopomp work on your own at home'! The voice was at the same time unequivocal and specific; it continued: 'You must do it every Friday afternoon at around two o'clock. And before you die you are to find someone younger with whom to do the work. Then, after you have returned to spirit, you will be able to carry on working jointly with this person while she (I *think*, but am not quite sure if the sex was made specific) is still on Earth.'

Well, I had been on umpteen workshops before and come away from them having made a good resolution, which I had then kept for at the very most three weeks. Yet somehow this time I knew that it was different. Whereas previous resolutions had come from my own (rather weak!) will, this was a very clear order from spirit, and orders from spirit clearly had to be obeyed. So the next evening, while waiting at Paddington Station in London for my train home, I felt prompted to purchase an exercise book in which to record my journeying experiences. I had the notion that listing my rescued souls on paper would encourage me to keep the weekly exercise up; it was only very much later that the idea of converting some of my notes into a book came to me.

Was that first psychopomp journey the start of a new career as a clairvoyant through whom spirit speaks? No, it was not! I have only received one unequivocal message since, and that was not more than a month after Simon Buxton's workshop. My husband and I, who were still busy recovering from the work involved in moving to a completely different part of England and settling into a new way of life following his retirement as a university professor, had for long had Peru at the top of our list of countries that we wanted to visit. I was also humming and hahing as to whether, when we did go to Peru, I would be up to doing the Inca Trail. Well, lying on the floor of my study on a Friday afternoon with the Michael Harner drumming escorting me through the 'dismemberment exercise' that I use as a prelude to my soul rescue journeys, the voice (or *a* voice!) came again. This time it said very firmly, 'Your trip to Peru is to be next year, and you're to do the Inca Trail.' I was again flabbergasted – especially since a trip to Peru was far from my mind at the time – but the voice continued: 'You need to walk the Trail in order to achieve some karmic balancing, and also there will be a project there that you'll want to support.' When I went downstairs a bit later and told David, 'We're going to Peru next year and we're going to do the Inca Trail', he replied, 'OK!' So I then set about making plans for the following October.

During the summer of 2005 we did as much walking in the hills around us as we could possibly fit in, and I went on the treadmill at our local sports center as often as I could bear it. Then, shortly before our departure, a friend told me about a project organized by a former neighbor of theirs – an archaeologist who was organizing the rebuilding of the channels that took water from the high Andes to the desert, following much destruction caused by guerrilla warfare. I therefore decided to have myself sponsored for doing the Trail, and the money I would raise for such a worthy cause was an added incentive for completing it. I was 65 at the time and, much though I love walking, I am not a physically strong person, and I was also considerably troubled by altitude sickness. Our wonderful Peruvian guide was, however, extraordinarily patient with my slow pace and I did, with great difficulty, complete the four-day Trail and was able to marvel at the site of Macchu Pichu when we finally arrived there.

I have never done a regression on the subject, but on the third day, when I was struggling particularly, I obtained the inner knowing (also hinted at by the voice in my head that had insisted on our doing the Trail) that I had been one of those responsible for the building of those amazing paths. I realized that I had been a male overseer, in a very strong body, and that I had had little or no patience with the workers whose bodies were weaker than my own. That is why I needed to achieve some 'karmic balance' by walking the Trail in a weak, feminine body. And soon after our return from Peru we heard that the Inca Trail had been closed for restoration. Hence the order from the 'all-knowing other side' to make the trip when we did!

Perhaps one day – who knows? – the need will arise for me to be given another order from spirit. In the meantime I simply carry on with my Friday afternoon excursions, trusting that I will be able to continue being of help to lost souls for quite a long time to come. During the eight years that I have been doing this work on my own I have so far completed, I am sorry to say, only 216 journeys. This is an indication of how often I have been either away from home on a Friday or impossibly busy, but I feel nevertheless that it is a large enough number from which to be able to write about my experiences with the aim of guiding others who may feel inspired to join in with this important work. I am sure that I have made it perfectly clear that I am not a qualified shaman, but part of my aim in writing on this subject is to demonstrate that *anyone* can be of help in this way. If I can do it, you who have picked up this book can most certainly learn to as well!

Our move to Ludlow, a town in South Shropshire in western England, was a case of 'love at first sight'. It was only *after* we had made the move from our house in the flat North East of England, where David's university is situated, that we found out all the reasons why Ludlow was such a good place for us to be living in. Its railway station was an obvious asset, and all the beautiful views were what had first attracted us, but, in addition to its excellent library and numerous cultural activities, the fact that it is such an old, historic town means that it is absolutely jam-packed full of ghosts. People who are more sensitive to such things than I am (of whom I know very many) might not want to live here for that very reason.

Being situated close to the border with Wales, Ludlow's castle – like others in the area – was built partly as defense from 'those dreadful Welsh' (apologies to my Welsh friends!), and it was for long the scene of innumerable battles. Not having the sensitivity of other people I know, it was only after I had started regularly making shamanic journeys that I became aware of the extent to which the inhabitants of this lovely town were literally surrounded by the ghosts of fighting soldiers who had never been told that their war was over. And that is not to mention the tormented souls who haunt some of the beautiful ancient dwellings and public houses. Not that my rescue work is by any means confined to the town in which I now live – once the drumming starts, one can let it transport one to anywhere in the world – but I came to appreciate why this place was so much in need of 'light workers' to make their homes here.

Now I have a very important point to make on the subject of trust. Some of you who read this may be quite different, but my experience as a regression therapist makes me believe that many people will be just like me in this way. During my therapy training it was constantly drummed into me to 'trust what comes', and the need to trust in whatever they see, hear, smell or feel is something that I always encourage in my own clients. Nevertheless, each time that I am performing a soul rescue journey, I am plagued by the feeling that it is all 'simply my imagination'. But spirit is good to me and so, every now and again, I am given sufficient confirmation to encourage me not to give up. For instance: I am no historian and, when I do hear bits of history, they tend to go into one ear and straight out of the other. So once, a few days after seeing on a journey a battle on Ludford Bridge (my favorite bridge in the whole world!), I was pleasantly surprised to read 'by chance' that some of the battles during the Wars of the Roses had been fought on that very bridge. On another occasion I rescued a soul who was trapped in the upper storey of the Buttercross, which is a historic building in the center of Ludlow. I am extraordinarily unobservant in some ways and, in all the many times that I had walked past the Buttercross, I had never noticed that it had an upper storey. So, on my next trip into the center of town, I made a point of looking, and sure enough I saw that the Buttercross was indeed a two-storey building!

More recently I heard from my friend Thia that a mutual acquaintance of ours called Kathy, who had just been widowed and does not use email, was being disturbed in the house by her husband Neil. So, on my next shamanic journey, I asked to be taken to the house, where I spoke to Neil. He had been suffering from heart trouble for many years before he died, and he told me that he could not imagine having a healthy heart and was feeling lost and confused. After I had helped him to cross over, I emailed Thia to tell her what had happened, but she was away on vacation at the time and so could only tell Kathy about it after her return. You can imagine my delight when Kathy herself called me to say that the disturbance in her house had ceased during Thia's absence!

So – just as I say to my Deep Memory Process clients! – TRUST that the rescue work you perform is real, not imaginary, and rest assured that you may eventually be thanked by some of the souls you help when you meet them again on the other side.

So now you have the story of how I personally came to be doing the fascinating work of rescuing lost souls. In the next chapter I shall outline the procedure – or rather *a* procedure –that can be followed. The shamanic is not the only possible method of performing soul rescue work and I can recommend, for instance, Wilma Davidson's book,[9] which is more broadly based than this one, covering many aspects of spirituality which I am here taking for granted. Her method is obviously effective, but you will soon see that the method I was taught, and have now been using for eight years, is equally so, as well as being very simple and straightforward. However, though I was particularly fascinated by her section on the healing abilities of animals, I do not personally agree with what Davidson describes as the use of 'white lies' to persuade lost souls to go to the light. My reservation about the 'white lies' is that it must surely hand over to the workers in higher realms some spirits who are rather difficult to deal with once the lie has been found out! Also, Wilma Davidson is a medium, which I am not, and my aim is to show that even those with no more than the average clairvoyant ability – something that we *all* have – can easily learn to do this work. I consequently disagree with Davidson's assertion that it is necessary to have mediumistic abilities in order to perform soul rescue work.

At this point a 'health warning' is perhaps called for. Firstly, this work is not to be recommended for unstable people or to anyone who suffers seriously from emotional or mental health problems. If in any doubt, it would be advisable to discuss the matter with your practitioner before attempting to do these sorts of exercises on your own. Secondly, even 'normal' people might find that they have unexpectedly powerful experiences. This does not at all mean that difficulties are to be anticipated – indeed they are rare – but one friend of mine, for instance, who is an experienced therapist, found on the first journey that she did on a shamanic workshop that she was shooting away from her body uncontrollably and had hastily to pull herself back. Someone less experienced than she was might have got herself into more serious difficulty. So, should you decide to plunge straight in to journeying without any prior preparation, it might be advisable to have a friend present just in case anything untoward happens.

In Part IV of the book I shall elaborate on the reasons that souls can get stuck in the astral realms, illustrating each example of a possible scenario from some of my own recorded 'case histories'. My learning in this field comes not only from these experiences, but also from my reading and my Deep Memory Process (DMP) work. Obviously my therapeutic training is very useful in this work, since souls who have left their physical bodies are no less in need of therapy than they were when they were still in them but, as I mentioned in my Introduction, I do not believe qualification as a therapist to be an essential prerequisite for the work. A reasonable amount of intelligence, combined with a good dose of common sense, is all that is really needed for counseling lost souls, explaining to them that they are 'dead', and pointing out to them that the time has now come for them to cross the river and find something much better. So now let us finish with introducing the subject and get down to the nitty gritty!

III

The Procedure

They linger in the shadow of the earth.
The earth's long conical shadow is full of souls
that cannot find the way across the sea of change.

Be kind, Oh be kind to your dead
and give them a little encouragement
and help them build their little ship of death...
D. H. Lawrence, 'All Souls' Day'

Spirit guides

Since for any sort of shamanic work it is essential to be aware of the spirit world, I should like to begin this section by talking about spirit guides. Richard Webster has an excellent book on contacting spirit guides and angels,[1] but I myself did not actually discover it until after I had tried various methods without a great deal of success. Where I personally have had more success in meeting them – and it was not even deliberate – was on shamanic journeys (about the only possible method that Webster does not mention!) and so I should now like to begin by introducing you to my own guides. This is not because any of them will be relevant to you personally, but simply to demonstrate the fact that an ordinary person like myself, without strong clairvoyant powers, can identify her own.

As Webster explains so well in his book, while it is our guardian angel who takes general care of us throughout the whole of our life(/lives), spirit guides are not angels but discarnate human beings who come to help us with specific tasks. They are often relatives or friends from a previous life, or even the present one, who are quite spiritually evolved and, not being incarnate, they are in a good position for seeing a broader picture of one's life and are consequently well equipped to give advice.

There are many books besides Webster's which give amazing stories of angel encounters, but I was also extremely interested in the statistics that Webster gives concerning accidents. He shows that research into such things as train crashes clearly indicates a tendency for trains that crash to have fewer passengers in them than would normally be expected! So is this not one of the best 'proofs' that could possibly be given for the workings of our spirit helpers? In fact, reading Webster's book suddenly reminded me of a somewhat strange experience that I had had some years previously. I was driving home from a regular visit to my homeopath on a road that I knew 'like the back of my hand', as we say. His clinic is well beyond York, about an hour and a half's drive from where I was living at the time, and we used to go to York frequently as well. Well, on that occasion I was driving along the A1079, which is the main road linking York and Hull in the north of England when, after a while, I suddenly became aware that I was no longer on the large main road, but on a minor road heading for Hebden Bridge in West Yorkshire (a place to which I had never been). I was not particularly tired or anything, and being on that road must have involved taking a left turn off the main one, which I had absolutely no recollection of doing. So, thinking about it again the other day, I asked my guardian angel whether he had made me do that in order to get me to avoid an accident, and he replied in the affirmative.

When I had my first reading from the renowned English clair-voyant Edwin Courtenay, he told me who my spirit guides were at that time, explaining that one normally had one 'permanent' guide throughout one's life, whereas the others would change according to the work one was doing. He described my permanent guide as Maria, a woman of letters to whom I had been married during the Elizabethan era, and told me that she was my writing guide. (I subsequently found for myself another lifetime in which she had been my wife.[2]) I no longer remember much about the other three guides that Edwin told me about, but that does not matter because they have since moved on.

For a few years I regretted my less frequent contact with Edwin, which I believed prevented me from getting updated on my spirit guides, but then I had a palm reading from a fellow Woolger graduate, who told me that my long-deceased father was coming in as one of my spirit guides and was interested in helping me to get my first book published. I was reluctant to believe this, firstly because during his lifetime my father would have greatly disapproved of my spiritual work, and secondly because I was still afraid of him. Another friend, however, encouraged me to work with the relationship, and once when I was unwell in bed, I suddenly saw a picture in my mind of a Turk with curly grey hair, twinkly eyes and a delightful smile. The idea that he might be my father as he had been in a previous life flashed into my feverish head and, when I dowsed for the answer, the reply that came was that we had in a Turkish lifetime been friends and colleagues. This made relating to my new guide a bit easier, but I was nevertheless not too distressed when he informed me during a meditation some time later that he had done all he could for me and was moving on to my youngest sister, who is also a healer and writer.[3] Then I gave little further thought to spirit guides until after my two workshops with Simon Buxton. In one of the very first journeys that I did on my own at home, I saw a nice-looking, middle-aged man with grey hair falling neatly below his ears and a headband going around his forehead. When I asked who he was, he replied that his task was to help me with my soul rescue work but, when I asked his name, he replied laughingly that I would not like it. So I insisted, and he then replied, 'George'. It is true that George had never been one of my favorite boys' names and, when I met him again the following week, he said that if I preferred I could call him by a name from one of his other incarnations – Ananda. Since Ananda means something akin to 'bliss' and I go to India regularly, this did indeed seem preferable and now, all these years on, I continue to invoke Ananda's assistance when I do soul rescue work (as well as with writing this book!).

Once I had started writing *Souls United*,[4] another guide appeared to me on a journey, who claimed to be an expert on the subject of twin-soulship. I have not yet established the nature of our previous connection, but she is a Peruvian named Amazon Flower, short and dumpy with a lovely broad smile. She saw me through to publication and, when she was gradually retiring, I asked to meet the guide who would be coming in to help with my book on adoption (which is as yet unfinished). The first time that I asked, I got a flash of a beautiful young woman in a long white dress, but had the impression that she was hovering in the background while the editing of *Souls United* was still in process. When, not long after, it appeared that the new guide was now coming in fully, she introduced herself as 'Ashtar' and explained that she had once fostered me when my own mother had been too poor to keep me. Then, when I was reworking my third book prior to getting it published, and doing a regression at a meeting with a group of fellow Woolger graduates, I met a large, cuddly man called Elahim, who told me that he had just come in to help me with the final stages of that book.

So those are my own spirit guides, but let me hasten to add that I just happen to be a very visual person. When I am regressed, I always get fairly vivid pictures, and sometimes I see a whole past life unfurl like a video. But not everyone is the same and, if you are not visual, there is no need to worry about it. Dr. Roger Woolger used to say that he was not visual at all, and that when he himself was regressed he got sounds and feelings rather than pictures. In fact he always stressed that feelings were the most important thing for DMP therapy, and so I am sure that the same holds true both for meetings with spirit guides and for soul rescue. If you know that mental pictures do not come easily to you, concentrate when you journey on noticing feelings, sounds, words or smells. These can all be equally valuable. And then, if you are still having trouble in identifying your guides, buy Richard Webster's book,[1] which I recommend anyway to anyone interested in this sort of topic!

Power animals

As I mentioned in the Introduction, we can make use of a power animal as well as a spirit guide to help us in rescuing lost souls. (In fact I believe that traditionally in shamanism more emphasis is put on animal helpers than on human ones.) In Simon Buxton's 'Way of the Shaman' workshops, he teaches how to find them as one journeys along a jungle river, explaining that it is not until it has appeared to you four times that you can be sure that a particular creature is your personal animal. When I attended that workshop in 2003, I was hoping for a brown bear, and also expecting it since that was the animal I had encountered on a previous workshop with the Norwegian Ivar Hajskfold, about whom I wrote in *Discovering the Life Plan*.[5] (And Ivar had told me that in his tradition the brown bear was all to do with writing and therapy!) I was not, however, at all distressed when my power animal at Buxton's workshop turned out to be a tiger, because one of my long-cherished ambitions (since achieved three-fold!) had been to spot a wild tiger in a national park in India. Nowadays, when I begin my shamanic journey by descending my spiral staircase to the River Teme in Ludlow, my boat is always awaiting me with both the tiger and the brown bear in it, but it is actually a snake that I have to follow along the path leading in turn to each of the souls that I am rescuing that day. I have to say that this gave me a real problem to start with, since I have had a horror of snakes all my life! However, on one of my many trips to India, I purchased in the street just outside Sai Baba's ashram in

Puttaparthi[6] a wooden snake made up of movable sections. He now sits coiled round one of the legs of Sai Baba's chair in my study, and I have gradually got used to his coming to life and transferring to my boat each time that I journey!

Preparation

Just as for any other spiritual work, it is important to use a 'sacred space'. For this reason I would strongly recommend always working in the same spot in your abode. A shaman will always start by cleansing the space in which he or she is going to work, and a traditional and simple way of doing this is by burning a bit of sage. (I have a large shell for holding a few sage leaves and, when I have put a match to them, I walk round my tiny study wafting the smoke into each corner.) Buxton at his workshops has people exercising vigorously to his drumming before starting on a journey (though I'm afraid I have to admit to being less vigorous when working on my own at home). Animal-like roars or screams are also recommended as part of the preparation exercise.

The drumming

The purpose of the drumming is to put oneself into a state of light trance, which will facilitate the traveling of one's mind. Obviously a real drum is ideal, and if you have one, or feel inspired to purchase one and to master this art, that is the method most highly recommended. Failing that, however, I find that the Michael Harner drumming CD which I purchased from the Sacred Trust[7] works admirably for me. It has two half-hour drumming sessions, and I use the first for an initial 'dismemberment' exercise and the second for the soul rescue journey. It is best to darken the room, and you will probably find a blindfold helpful. (I use one of those that are sometimes given out by airlines.) Lying comfortably on one's back is the norm, but remember that comfort is the priority, so do whatever you find suits you.

Dismemberment

Shamans are always very well aware that we are not our bodies, and so 'dismemberment' is an easy way to remember this and to strip us of our ego, which is obviously useful for performing spiritual work. I consequently see this little exercise as an excellent preliminary to the important work of soul rescue. Everyone can devise their own personal method, but this is what I do. Being greatly enamored of Malidoma Somé's wonderful autobiography *Of Water and the Spirit*,[8] I visualize a burning hoop such as he had to jump through at the beginning of his initiation. What happens varies from week to week, but after I have run along a path flanked on both sides by African warriors and jumped through the hoop (somehow avoiding the flames!), my physical body is always attacked immediately. Often I plunge straight into deep water, where I might get instantly swallowed by a whale, or nibbled by a host of small fish; sometimes eagles or other large birds swoop down and start pecking away at me, or rip off whole limbs in a trice. Equally often I meet a group of my beloved tigers, who of course do what comes naturally to them when coming face to face with a human being. Whatever happens, I then lose little time in soaring out of my body and up on to a cloud, where I often find Sai Baba (the avatar of our age and for long my own 'guru') and/or one or two of my spirit guides waiting for me. I then chat to them about whatever happens to be most on my mind that day, and normally I receive consolation or encouragement. (NB: This, like my conversations with my spirit guides, comes in the form of thoughts in my head rather than the clear voice that I heard on the two occasions I described previously.) When the drumming speeds up, it is the signal that it is time to return, and it is important to remember to collect your body on the way back and get it hastily put together again. You can then, if you like, have a pause in order to reflect on what has just happened and/or make notes, or else you can go straight into the psychopomp.

Descent into the underworld

At the 'Way of the Shaman' workshop we were taught both ascent and descent. If you are wanting to, say, meet your spirit guide(s), then you should go up, since they dwell, metaphorically speaking, in 'higher' realms. Whereas for psychopomp you have to descend to the 'underworld' because lost souls have not yet reached the 'higher' realms. Both directions are equally simple to master, and it is entirely up to the individual to choose his or her own preferred routes. You can, for instance, go up a mountain or down a rabbit hole, up a tree or down through its trunk. If you are wanting to meet a spirit guide, all you need to do is to go up your mountain/tree/staircase or whatever you have chosen and then sit down and ask him or her to come to you. If it doesn't work the first time, just be patient and keep trying. ('Practice makes perfect!')

As I mentioned already, for the psychopomp work, I go down a spiral staircase to a boat waiting in the larger of Ludlow's two rivers, but you might prefer, for instance, a deep cave. But whatever you choose, once you have made your choice, don't change it. You will find after a very few weeks of regular journeying that the process becomes completely automatic. I find that the second the drumming starts I am shooting down the staircase like a rocket without even consciously willing it. I then find that the speed with which I begin my encounters varies from week to week. Don't worry about that; just let go and let whatever is intended happen. Remember that you are working together with spirit, that you are no more than a humble assistant to beings who have a broader overview, and so let them take charge. You may well be surprised at how quickly it starts to go well for you. I usually complete between about four and eight encounters during my half-hour, but again it varies according to the needs of the individual lost souls.

The next steps

I. *Listen to the lost soul's story*

Remember that the souls that you meet are truly suffering. How much they are suffering depends entirely upon their level of awareness, but a sympathetic ear can never come amiss. Even if a soul is aggressive or angry, you have nothing to fear because you are well protected. (Simon Buxton, as I said, teaches use of power animals for protection, but when I went to a talk by the well-known shaman and author Manda Scott, she said that she did not use power animals. You can use your own preferred form of protection.) The story they tell you may seem totally ridiculous or nonsensical, but it is their reality, in which they may well have been trapped for hundreds of years, so just do your best to be understanding and empathetic and make it clear that you are simply there to offer help, not to judge or condemn.

2. *Explain the situation*

There are many exceptions, but as a general rule the souls that you meet are completely unaware that they have died. Once you have clarified how they died, you can explain to them what happened and give them some sort of proof. (I normally get a picture straight away showing how they died, but it will no doubt be different for a non-visual person.) For instance: when it is a Ludlow ghost, I often take them out into the town to show them how it has changed, pointing out such things as cars, which of course normally did not exist when they were last in a physical body. Often they are plagued by thought forms of, say, animals that are tormenting them. In such cases show the person how you can simply blow the thought forms away. If they have fallen down a well, or drowned in a river or the sea, you can start by grabbing them by the hand and pulling them to safety. Sometimes people are ashamed of their crippled or aged body. Then you can teach them how to change their appearance at will, simply by imagining the sort of body they would like to have. You will find that you can give lost souls many pleasant surprises!

If any of these ploys still fails to convince a soul that he or she is dead, then it is time to bring in the trump card – the card which needs to be used at the final stage anyway. Ask the person you are dealing with to think of someone they cared about whom they know to be dead, and then call upon them. (Even the saddest, most unloved people will usually be able to think of *someone*; it might as a last resort even be a pet dog or cat.) The immediate appearance of the spirit called upon will normally bring both joy and an understanding that something has changed for the soul concerned.

One of the many things that I have learned on my spiritual journey (and that is well explained in the fictional final chapter of my third book[5]) is that, when one dies, one finds what one expects to find. So a committed Christian is likely to meet Jesus, a Buddhist the Buddha, a Muslim Allah, and so on. Atheists, on the other hand, will expect to find nothing when they die, and so that is exactly what does happen. Fortunately no soul is left to stagnate in nothingness indefinitely, but waking them up can sometimes take a lot of hard work. For this reason spiritual education during a lifetime can save a lot of time after the end of it!

3. Offer counseling as necessary and appropriate

The counseling will again vary immensely according to individual circumstances. Frequently people are ashamed of something they have done, and that is what is keeping them stuck. In such cases it is important to get them to forgive themselves, however hard it may seem to them. This does not of course necessitate condoning horrendous crimes, but you can tell them that (contrary to what the Church taught so many of us) God does not judge; that we ourselves are the only judges.

Anger can be even more difficult to deal with, but you can gently point out that being stuck in anger is only making them unhappy and that it is time to let go of it. Trying to get over the point of view of the person with whom they are angry sometimes helps. In really hopeless cases, the main thing is to get the soul to cross over and, once he or she has done that, you can safely leave them in the care of wiser beings.

In Part IV I give various examples of further possible scenarios and how they can be dealt with. The main thing is to be guided by your intuition. It is most unlikely that you would have picked up this book if you were not the sort of person with a natural talent for this type of work.

4. The final rescue

Once you feel you have given a soul all the help that you are able, it is time for them to be encouraged to cross over. Quite often I find myself telling them not to worry about something, since they will have a chance to deal with it in a future life. Very often I tell them how much better they will find things to be for them once they have made the transition. Then, when they are ready, all you need to do is ask them to think of a relative or friend who is dead and call for them. Once the spirit has appeared – and this is invariably speedy – you can watch your lost soul being led to safety, and you can then move on to the next one.

So, now it is time for illustration from some of my own case histories. I have given them all names, but many of these are fictitious because it was only after I had decided to write this book that I began to make a regular habit of asking my lost souls their names. You may or may not wish to bother with names when doing your own work. You may even wish to either join or form a soul rescue group. Living where I do, this has not proved possible for me, but group work always has extra power as well as giving one an added incentive. Good luck anyway, and remember to stick at it!

IV

The Reasons Why Souls Get Stuck on the Earth's Plane

For the soul has a long, long journey after death
to the sweet home of pure oblivion.
Each needs a little ship, a little ship
and the proper store of meal for the longest journey.
D. H. Lawrence, 'All Souls' Day'

I. Accidents

Often when people are killed in, for instance, a car crash, they do not, as we have seen, have time to realize that they have died. And since, as I explained earlier, the 'astral realms' look exactly the same as the world we know here, they need help for the realization to dawn. I imagine that there can be nothing more frustrating for a soul to go home and find that none of his or her family is aware of their presence! In my second book[1] I wrote about a very spiritual twin-soul couple named Ann and Ken Evans. Ken, who was an artist, communicated with Ann regularly after he had died, and (though he has apparently since moved on to 'higher planes') he told her initially that his work was explaining to people who had just died very suddenly that they were dead, and helping them to cross over. He used art therapy in his work, but, again as I said earlier, spirit workers on the other side also need the assistance of someone on Earth to help souls to cross over. I have in my own practice found many people who were stuck after dying in accidents.

On 9 August 2011, I was driving my husband and daughter to an interesting place in North Shropshire called Hawkstone Park. On the way there we were fortunate to miss – possibly by seconds, certainly by no more than a very few minutes – being involved in a very serious accident on a rather narrow stretch of the A49 just north of Shrewsbury. We came upon a jeep that was upside down in the middle of the road, and a small car, which was badly smashed and smoking, was perched precariously over a drop on the right-hand side of the road. By the time we got there, a few people were standing around making telephone calls, and a woman was extricated from the jeep before any professional assistance arrived on the scene. In due course we were directed to turn round and take another route, and on our return home later in the day we found that bit of the A49 to be still closed. Concerned about those involved in the accident, I purchased the local paper the next day to find out more. From this I learned that, though the two drivers had miraculously survived (and fortunately neither vehicle had any passengers), there had been a fatality at that very spot one week previously. So, suspecting an 'accident black spot', I went there on my next journey. I found that the 25-year-old victim (whose name I do not wish to divulge for obvious reasons) was not only very lost and confused, but also very angry about his collision with an ambulance. It took me some time to convince him that his life in that particular body was now over, and it was also clear that he was very ignorant of anything remotely spiritual. After we had talked for a bit, he expressed further anger about the death from drug abuse of his friend Wayne. Wayne himself then appeared, also lost, but the two were delighted to be reunited and that made dispatching them both a bit easier. Wayne called for his father, and the ambulance victim called for his grandfather, so now I sincerely hope that the bit of the A49 near Wem will not be an accident 'black spot'.

A bit nearer my own home and a bit longer ago was Tom, a young man who had just been killed in a car accident on the A49 road that bypasses Ludlow. It seemed that he *had* appreciated that his injuries were fatal but, since he also did not believe in the afterlife, I had to shake him awake initially, which gave him something of a shock. However, after we had talked for a bit about there really being no such thing as death, he happily called for his deceased grandmother.

Road accidents are alas numerous, but I prefer to turn now to examples of other sorts of accidents. To quote Wikipedia, the Indian Ocean earthquake that occurred on 26 December 2004 was caused by subduction and was an undersea megathrust earthquake with an epicenter off the west coast of Sumatra, Indonesia. Known by the scientific community as the Sumatra–Andaman earthquake, it triggered a series of devastating tsunamis along the coasts of most landmasses bordering the Indian Ocean and killed over 230,000 people in 14 countries. It inundated coastal communities with waves up to 30 meters high and was one of the deadliest natural disasters in recorded history. Indonesia was the hardest-hit country, followed by Sri Lanka, India and Thailand. It is therefore hardly surprising that much of my psychopomp time over the ensuing weeks was devoted to helping tsunami victims. I will mention just a few of them.

Chanarong was a young Thai boy – I'm afraid I Googled for the Thai names rather than asking the souls! – who was desperately looking for his mother. Fortunately we found her and she had also failed to cross over on account of the fact that she was busy looking for *him*. Once they had been reunited they were able to cross over straight away, and the mother collected up some other lost children as well. On this same journey that I did shortly after the tsunami, I also met three Hindu priests in India who were so good at meditating that they had been in trance and unaware of having been swept away! I told them that they had a great gift, but pointed out that a monk really ought to be able to tell the difference between being alive and dead. They immediately saw the point and moved on.

In these two cases it was not necessary for the deceased to call upon someone from the other side to collect them because they were all able to realize for themselves that they were dead and the consequent need to cross over. On the other hand, Isra (I think that's the right name!), a little Indonesian girl whose mother was still alive, did not know at all what to do. Once I had explained to her that her mother was still on Earth and could rejoin her at night when her soul left her body, she was able to call for her grandmother whom she knew to be dead.

Six young Sri Lankan boys who had been playing together when they were swept away by the tsunami were terrified because they could not swim. So all that I needed to do was to show them how they could float up out of the water and that convinced them that they had left their physical bodies. One then called for his grandmother, the next for his mother, who had died some time previously, the next for a deceased aunt, and the last two, who were twins, called for their grandmother.

The severe earthquake in Christchurch in 2011 also of course caused a lot of confusion among those who lost their lives, and on my journeys I went there repeatedly as well. When I met Amanda, a 4-year old girl who did not understand at all what had happened, I was able to enlist some angels to help her, but the 10-year-old Bernard and his 8-year-old brother had been fighting each other when the earthquake struck and so they saw it as 'God's punishment'. Once I had assured them that this was not the case and that, when they had crossed over, they would be able to console their grieving parents, they called for their deceased grandmother. A group of Maoris, on the other hand, had a very good understanding of what had happened, and so they indicated to me a group of four men who had been drunk inside a pub when it had collapsed on top of them. Once I had convinced these men that it was time to wake up and cross over, they were each able to call for a deceased parent or grandparent.

The year 2011 of course saw another severe tsunami, and so last year I went to Japan several times as well. On the first occasion I met a mother who was frantic at having lost her child and, since they were both dead, I was able to reunite them, explain what had happened, and get the mother to call for her mother to take them across. A group of six schoolgirls were still happily skipping together without having realized what had happened, so again an explanation was called for and, once persuaded that they were dead, they each called for a deceased relative. A little bit more difficult to deal with were firstly the hundred or so passengers in a boat that had got completely swept away, and secondly a schoolmaster who was still trying to control his class. But I hope that I succeeded in getting through to them all about what had happened and why they needed to call for someone on the other side.

Much nearer home was James, whose death had been rather longer ago. He had been killed by a brick landing on his head when workers were building Ludlow's Assembly Rooms. He was fairly newly married and so had got very upset when he had gone home and his wife had 'ignored' him. This of course happens to many souls who want to communicate with their loved ones. If they do not realize that they are dead, they cannot appreciate that they are invisible! James was afraid that his wife's reason for ignoring him was that she had got interested in someone else, but once I had explained the situation to him, he was happy to call for his grandmother.

Although very often people who die quickly in accidents do not have time to realize that they are dead, this was not quite the case with Lucille, whose head hit a rock when she dived into the River Rhône in Geneva. At one level she was aware of having left her body, but at the same time she felt angry and frustrated because she believed herself to be too young to die, and it was this that was holding her trapped on the Earth's plane. I was therefore able to console her by telling her about reincarnation – that she would be able to return to Earth in another body – and then she was happy to call for her deceased grandmother.

2. Ignorance

This of course takes many forms. Often it is simply that people (like the car victims mentioned above) do not believe in the immortality of the soul. Ollie, for instance, was a tramp/hobo, whom I found to be sound asleep after having died of hypothermia. So my first task was to wake him and, when I had done that, he said that he did not believe in an afterlife or in God because, if there were a God, He would not let anyone be homeless and die of cold. I pointed out that there must be an afterlife since he was now awake and talking to me, to which he replied that he must have made a mistake and had not died after all. So then, after giving him proof that he was dead, I explained to him about karma and that he would not need to be homeless in his next life. When I asked if he wanted to call for his mother, who had died some time before him, he replied negatively since his mother had been an alcoholic, but I then succeeded in getting him to call for his grandmother and he went off happily with her.

Elspeth, who was in love with a soldier called Henry, would not give up waiting for him to return from a war. While she was waiting, Eric fell in love with her and tried to persuade her to accept him instead. When she refused to do so, he got so enraged that he killed her, but she simply carried on waiting for her beloved to return, not having noticed that she had been killed. I saw the story and was thus able to convince her that both she and Henry were long since dead, and so she was then more than happy to call for him.

Bertram was a soldier in Ludlow who had been killed in a battle, but had got stuck simply because he did not believe in the afterlife. On getting up from the grass and realizing that his Christian fellows had been right about immortality, he expected to see a bloody body on the ground. However, once I had led him into the center of town and shown him how much it had changed, he appreciated how much time had passed and that his body had long since been buried. It was then easy to get him to call for his grandmother.

The world, alas, never seems to be free of war, but at the moment this is in the Middle East rather than Europe. Egypt is hopefully recovering from the 2011 political uprising, but early in 2012 there was a terrible incident on a football ground in which many people were killed. I came across a dozen men who were still fighting, even though they did not really seem to know exactly what they were fighting about. So I told them that they had all been killed, pointed out the futility of their actions, and then persuaded them all to call for a deceased relative or friend.

Jeffrey's was a different sort of ignorance. A drunken brawl had taken place in the house in which he lived and worked as a servant, and he had been stripped of his clothes because his employers thought he was hiding some gold that had gone missing. He did have a vague idea about having been killed, but thought he could not possibly go out without his clothes on. So I helped him to find some clothes to put on and, once he felt respectable, he was happy to call for his grandmother.

Amy had such a cruel husband that she had finally thrown herself off Ludford Bridge in Ludlow, but his words, 'You can never escape me', had become so firmly ingrained in her consciousness that she had become stuck in the River Teme. She also felt guilty about having at one point in her marriage taken a lover and so needed a good deal of consoling and encouragement. Peter, the lover, had died (possibly from poisoning by the husband, though Amy had no proof of that), and so it was lovely for me to see them reunited once she had plucked up the courage to call for him.

Brainwashing either by the Church, by parents or by someone else is a frequent cause of ignorance. On another occasion I met a 'ghost', who turned out to be a young girl named Helena who had often pretended to be a ghost by dressing herself up in a sheet. Her mother had told her, 'If you keep dressing up as a ghost, you'll turn into one!', and she had died of pneumonia at the age of 20. So I showed Helena that she only needed to remove the sheet in order to stop being a ghost, and pointed out that it would be much better to move on than to upset people on Earth. She was easily convinced and called for her father.

A very sad case of enforced ignorance was a little orphaned African boy, who had been brought up in a community that was 100% white. His carers had nicknamed him Little Black Sambo, and told him that only white people could go to Heaven. After accepting my assurance that this was nonsense and that there were in fact many more black people in Heaven than white, he summoned his parents, who called him something that sounded to me like Malibongo. The mother was very fat with broad hips; she had a very small child on one hip and she simply picked Malibongo up and carried him off on her other hip.

Another African child was a little girl who had been eaten by a crocodile. She was shouting from inside the crocodile, believing that she could never escape. This, I think, was another case of parental brainwashing, and I told her that the etheric crocodile was friendlier than the physical one and that it would simply cough her up again if I asked it to. The crocodile promptly did that and then apologized to the child, explaining that its physical body had needed sustenance. She was then told about karma and shown a previous life in which she had been a man who had killed many crocodiles. This made her understand the reason for what had happened to her and she then called for her mother.

In 2006 my husband and I went to Canada, where we had the good fortune to take the Rocky Mountaineer train from Banff to Vancouver. On the journey we passed a derelict TB hospital, which our guide explained to us had proved impossible to sell after it had fallen out of use on account of the ghosts inhabiting it. So after my return home, I journeyed there and met, firstly, Bert, an old man in pajamas who thought he could not go anywhere because of the fear of spreading infection. It was only necessary to explain to him that he had died, and that there was no risk of infection on the other side, for him to be sufficiently relieved to call for his father. Jemima, who was trapped in the hospital's underground passage, was also easy to deal with and promptly called for her mother. A little more difficult was Alf, who was upset at the disease having rendered it impossible for him to climb one of the Rocky Mountains. But once I had assured him that he would be able to make another attempt in a future lifetime, he called for a fellow climber whose death had grieved him greatly.

Anil was an Indian 'guru' figure whose ignorance was of a very different sort. He had become so big-headed that he thought it his 'duty' to go on and on preaching to the 'ignorant' and was surrounded by a group of a dozen or so people who had obviously been listening to him non-stop for very many years. He was so busy that he had not noticed that he had died. I asked him whether he believed himself to be immortal, to which he replied negatively, but said that he did expect to have a very long life. He was offended when I suggested that his life might have already ended, but I assured him that I had been studying these things in depth and knew what I was talking about! Eventually I convinced him that his body was only etheric, not physical, by showing that I could put my hand straight through it. He then called for his own guru, who told me that, after he himself had died, his pupil Anil had got carried away with self-importance.

3. Guilt

Guilt is an extremely common cause of souls getting stuck and I am here mentioning only a small number of the very many examples I have met. Eric, who had killed Elspeth, was of course also long dead, but he was so consumed with guilt about having murdered the girl he loved that this prevented him from feeling able to cross over. As we always find in DMP therapy, self-forgiveness is the hardest thing of all, but in Eric's case my being able to tell him that his victim was now reunited with the man she really loved made it possible for him to do this. He then plucked up the courage to call for his deceased mother.

I came across another murder in a temple in Egypt, but in this case the man concerned, Arafa, had killed a young boy because (for some reason that was not made clear to me) he believed it to be his duty. Only on dying had he realized that it had been wrong, and so again it was guilt that had made him get stuck.

The genuine belief that the crime had been committed out of supposed duty made it a bit easier for Arafa to forgive himself, and he was then willing to call for his mother.

Terry was consumed with guilt for quite a different reason. He had been killed in a car crash after drinking too much and, since he realized that it had been a big mistake to try and drive home when he had known perfectly well that he was over the limit, he was still trapped in 'no man's land'. Self-forgiveness, as I have said, is always the hardest thing, but I did manage to persuade Terry that his behavior was no worse than that of many young men and (also like many young men) he had a deceased grandmother of whom he had been fond to call for.

The 20-year-old Dave felt guilty because he happened to have been skiving from work when the 2011 Christchurch earthquake struck. It turned out that his office had been completely obliterated anyway, which meant that he would still have died if he had been at work. So I explained that we all had multitudinous lives of differing length and told him that it had clearly been his destiny to die young this time. That helped him to forgive himself and he then called for his grandfather.

Another very different sort of case was that of the poor child Lily, who was absolutely heartbroken at the death of her puppy, Jasmine. She was also consumed with guilt because the dog had

been run over through her fault. (Her mother had ordered her not to let it off the lead.) It was not clear how Lily herself had died, but she was easy to help because she was so delighted when I told her that she could call for Jasmine (who she firmly told me was male!). The dog then led the delighted little girl across to the other side.

Charlie was a little boy who had got lost in the forest and stolen a loaf of bread. Even though he was hungry, he felt guilty because he knew it was wrong to steal. He would not even start eating it until he had found his twin sister to share it with, so the bread had gone moldy and he had died of starvation. We restored the loaf to its original pristine whiteness and then Charlie called for his sister, who had in the interim grown to adulthood, but she rejuvenated herself so that he would recognize her. Then, in order to please him, she ate the bread with him before leading him away.

Just five minutes' walk from our house in Ludlow there is a wonderful dog-walking area, which is now officially named 'Millennium Green' but is in fact still known to everyone in the locality by its traditional name of 'Gallows Bank'. I have always assumed that the large stone at the top of the hill is the spot where the gallows were situated, and it has never surprised me to be taken there on a psychopomp journey. Rodney, who I think was hung on Gallows Bank at some point during the late Middle Ages, was still feeling guilty about his 'life of crime'. Since this had really only been prompted by poverty, it was not too difficult to get him to forgive himself and call for his mother.

Ellen, who had been a prostitute, was perhaps hanged slightly more justifiably than Rodney, since she had stolen money from a wealthy client. It was easy to empathize with her too, though, because she was only wanting to escape from her life of prostitution and better herself. So again I persuaded her to forgive herself and call for her mother.

Moving again a long way away from Ludlow, I met Harold, a

sailor, who believed when he died that he would be punished on account of having a wife in each of the ports to which he called. He actually preferred the wife in New York, but felt very guilty about the English one, whom he had married first. After I had assured him that there was no marriage on the other side, that he needed to forgive himself, and that he could apologize to the first wife when he met her again, he called for his grandfather.

Simon was a cyclist who had lived in Geneva, rather more recently. He had crashed a red light (something that we observed cyclists doing a lot when we were last in Geneva in the summer of 2011!) and had consequently knocked down a pedestrian. I found out that, though the pedestrian had had to go to hospital, he was now fully recovered. Fortunately that alleviated Simon's feelings of guilt sufficiently to enable him to call for his great-grandfather.

4. Fear

Fear is endemic in the human condition, but it is a serious obstacle to spiritual growth and happiness. And since fear, which can of course be caused by many different things, is another very common preventive to crossing over after death, it seems highly desirable to do all one can to conquer it while one is still alive. Does not the Bible say that 'love casteth out fear'?[2] This may sound simple, but any therapist will tell you that it is rarely so. Often our fears are buried too deep for us to be aware of them, and this is why a therapy such as Deep Memory Process can sometime be so useful. My own conquest of deep-seated fears, combined with my discovery of the reality of divine Love, has been greatly helped by DMP, and I have also been the joyful witness of the shedding of much fear among my own incarnate clients. Many of the discarnate ones too have had to be helped to shed their fear before they could cross over.

Priya and Chetan were a young couple in India who were in

love and had run off together to escape from the marriages that each of their families had chosen for them. Unfortunately Chetan had been killed by a tiger and then, in her distress, the young girl had killed herself with his sword. They were stuck because they did not want either to face the wrath of their families or be separated. I assured them both that there would not be any wrath on the other side and that, once they had crossed over, they could prepare to reincarnate in a country in which marriages were not arranged. After that they had no need to call for assistance because they were ready to walk through a door which they could see had light coming through it from the other side. Being Indian, they no doubt had a better idea of what happens when one leaves the body than do many Westerners.

Leila and Alfred, for instance, were a couple in Ludlow who had not dared to return home on account of the Welsh having invaded the town! I found them stuck in a boat on the River Corve. Fortunately I only needed to take them into the town and show them how things had changed for their fears to be dissipated. (Dispelling fear in 'Earthly' therapy often takes much longer!) This couple then lost no time in calling for one of their parents.

Another easy case was that of Diana, a young girl in Ludlow who was constantly being scolded for her 'wrongdoings'. Consequently, when she swallowed something poisonous, she did not dare to tell anyone that she was feeling ill. So we wound back to her funeral in order to help her understand what had happened, and then she called for her great-grandmother.

Naomi was a young girl who was scared to meet her father because she had disobeyed him and spat out her medicine, which tasted foul. She thought that was why she had died, but we were told that in fact it was not doing her any good and that her sickness had been bound to kill her anyway. A snake came to show her the way, but Naomi was scared of snakes. So I told her that this etheric one was different from the snakes she had seen in the zoo and was actually a symbol of healing. This encouraged her to follow the snake and call for her grandmother, of whom she was fond.

Another child I met was little Joe in Alaska, who had been eaten by a bear. He had gone off into the mountains because his friends had been teasing him about his fear of bears and he wanted to prove them wrong. When the bear had dashed his head on the ground, he had died too quickly to realize what had happened and so was still wandering through the mountains afraid of a bear coming. I found that the bear was now waiting to apologize to Joe and, once it had explained to him that it had been hungry, they had a lovely 'bear hug'. Joe was then ready to call for his deceased grandmother to come and rescue him.

Bertie was another child who was scared to meet his parents after being disobedient. He'd been brought up to be neither seen nor heard, and I found him hiding under a dining table at which the rest of his family were sitting eating. He had died when he had escaped from the house and been kicked by a horse. The poor child had no inkling of love, and so I gave him a cuddle to show him that that was what children needed rather than punishment. Then I explained that I could not look after him since I had work to do on Earth, but told him that there were plenty of mother figures on the other side who would love to take care of him. One such came without Bertie himself needing to think of someone to call for, and he was delighted to go off with her.

I have come across many people who have died from drowning. Harry, for instance, who could not swim, was absolutely terrified when he had been blown into a pond in a gale. I found him treading water and wondering how he could ever escape. I pulled him out and sat down with him on the bank for quite a while before eventually convincing him that he was dead. Once convinced, he did not hesitate in calling for his mother.

From my experience death by drowning appears to prevent many people crossing over. I encountered Victor simply sitting at the bottom of the sea because he realized that (despite his name!) he had failed totally in his Life Plan. I persuaded him that it would be okay to cross over since nobody on the other side would judge him. His great-grandfather, whom he had known briefly as a child, was the only person he could remember having ever shown him any love, so he called for him.

5. Responsibility

Feelings of responsibility are important but, if taken too far, they can sometimes be a hindrance in the journey back to the Source for which we are all aiming, whether or not we are aware of it. Roger Woolger used to talk often of releasing whole armies who were attached to a client he was treating because their leader (a general or the equivalent) had not realized that the war was over and felt responsible for his men. I have no such experience, but Ludlow, as I mentioned before, has been the scene of numerous battles, and once when I was on a psychopomp journey I suddenly felt very cold. (This was not by any means the only time that I have experienced bodily sensations caused by the atmosphere of the place I am visiting.) During the Middle Ages Ludlow, like many British towns, was completely surrounded by a wall, and I saw that the town was enveloped in snow and a soldier, whose job it was to guard the town, was walking along the top of this wall. He was obviously suffering severely from the cold, but felt unable to leave his post in spite of the snow. So I led him down off the wall and showed him firstly that it was no longer snowing in Ludlow and secondly that very little of the wall still remained. That helped to convince him that he was dead and no longer needed in his important job, and he then called for his one-time lover. She was on the other side of the River Teme and she rowed across in a boat to collect him.

Much of the walls of the English city of York, on the other hand, are still intact, and there I once encountered a soldier named Benjamin who had been shot dead by an arrow but still thought that he must carry on defending York. This was another case where it was not difficult to convince the soldier that he was dead by pointing out how much change had occurred during the intervening centuries, and he then willingly called for his grandmother.

Very often on my journeys I encounter groups of soldiers who

are still fighting because nobody has told them either that the war is over or that they have been killed. When I give them the very out-of-date news that their battle has ended, I rarely find that the whole group is willing to listen, but fortunately a good proportion of them usually do stop and hear what I am saying, and then it is not too difficult to point out the changes that have taken place in the town. This will then convince them that there is no need to persevere with the fighting and that it would be a good idea to cross over. Ludlow is of course not unique, and I have also on occasion intervened in battles near Shrewsbury and other places either in England or elsewhere.

A rather different sort of case of responsibility involved the captain of a sailing ship. At the beginning of 2011, my husband and I were in Australia and we did a four-day Whitsunday Island trip on the wonderful *Solway Lass*, which was originally built in 1902 and has a fascinating history. This ship underwent a series of incidents of varying gravity; they included being captured by the Germans during World War Two and having to be beached after striking two mines. Our captain told us that she was said to be haunted by a previous captain and so naturally, on a subsequent shamanic journey, I endeavored to meet him. This endeavor was successful and the 'ghost' captain told me that he felt responsible for the sufferings of his crew. I assured him that they were all fine now and, after convincing him that he was dead, told him that he was now free to do other things. He had no interest in anything other than working on a boat and so, since he did not fancy a larger, faster boat such as I told him were prevalent nowadays, I suggested other things to do with boats that he might like to do. Then I explained that before returning to Earth in a new body he would first need to cross over to the other side and, when I asked him about someone important to him who was dead, he called for Joseph, the man who had taught him to sail.

Returning again to Ludlow, Margaret was a housekeeper in a

large house owned by a big family who had many servants. It was her job to keep order in the house and she was very conscientious about her responsibilities. Only after I had shown her that no one apart from an elderly couple was living there now, was she willing to relinquish her duties. Her mother then came quickly when called.

Eileen had lost her baby, feared that it had died and was so consumed by the responsibilities of motherhood that she did not think about the fact that she herself had also died. But once I had helped her to find the baby, she was happy to take it across to the other side herself.

Going back for a moment to the well-remembered Boxing Day tsunami, Jan, a Scandinavian who was working and living with his family in Indonesia, was in the aftermath of the tsunami desperately worried about his orphaned son. (His wife was not in sight, but I think she had already crossed over.) When I asked whether he did not have any family who could look after the boy, he replied that he had a sister who was fond of him, but that she was in Scandinavia. I pointed out that (sadly!) a white person would more easily get help than most of the native Indonesians, and he agreed with me. Then, when I had explained that he would be better able to help his son if he crossed over and joined his wife, he called for his grandmother.

A slightly similar case was an Indonesian grandfather, who had promised to buy his granddaughter some marbles when he could afford them. Since the little girl's father was clearly dead and her mother was lost, it seemed that she would ultimately be adopted – probably by an American family. Once I had told the old man that the adoptive family would be able to afford some marbles for the child, he was happy to go, and he then called for his fairly long-deceased wife.

Marion and George were a wonderful couple, who had started a soup kitchen for the homeless after the first earthquake in Christchurch and had enlisted four helpers. All six were too involved in their valuable work to be concerned about being dead themselves, and so I had to explain that they were no longer needed there but could be of greater use if they crossed over. I further told them that they were obviously qualified to go to a high realm since they were thinking purely about helping others. Once the situation became clear to them, they each had a parent or grandparent to call for.

A similar case was of a young Syrian nurse (called, I think, something like Isara) who was desperately upset about the constant killings and woundings in her country and having too many people to deal with. I explained to her that, including herself, a whole group of people in the ward she was working in had been killed by a bomb and that things would be better when she had crossed over. She was keen to meet Allah so, when I had assured her that she would be able to do so, she called for her grandmother.

Not long after Christchurch had had its second earthquake, the world was shaken again by the Japanese 2011 tsunami. I have always been against nuclear power and felt sad when people did not seem to have learned from Chernobyl. Will they now learn from Fukushima in Japan, where so many people had to be evacuated and the school children who survived still have to wear gadgets round their necks to measure their levels of radiation? There I met Hosui, who was trying desperately to fix the nuclear problem. He was employed there when the radiation caused his death, and felt both guilty and responsible on account of having been one of the biggest protagonists of the Fukushima plant. I succeeded in convincing him that he would be able to do more to help if he crossed over, and so he then called for his father, whom he described as 'a man to be proud of'.

Yet another form of responsibility can often be found in the Church. Once when I was just starting off on my psychopomp journey, I was greeted by a cry of 'There's been a murder in Hereford Cathedral!' It turned out that a prelate named John had been executed for his 'heretical views' (which I think were probably Cathar-type leanings), and the criminal had got off undetected and become Bishop Trevor. I found the bishop still stalking the cathedral, 'guarding it against further heresy'. As happens so frequently, all I needed to do to convince him that he was dead, and therefore wasting his time, was to point out the changes that had taken place in Hereford during the intervening centuries. This did not of course make him happy about the 'heretics', but it did cause him to call for his mother to take him 'to Heaven'.

Finally, in contrast to any of the above, I once met a zookeeper in China who was stuck with his pandas because of fearing their extinction. Once I had explained that he could help more in their predicament by crossing over, he called for a deceased colleague.

6. Attachment to worldly pursuits

In my second book, *Souls United*,[1] I wrote about Richard Burton and Elizabeth Taylor, but there my interest was in their extraordinary relationship, which has every appearance of being a twin-soul one. Much more recently I was fascinated to see on television a repeat of an interview that Michael Parkinson gave Richard Burton in 1974, shortly after his first divorce from Taylor and about ten years before he died. A better example of someone who succumbed to *all* the temptations of Earthly life would be hard to find, and one thing that greatly interested me in hearing Richard speak about himself was his total frankness and honesty. Still renowned as one of the greatest actors of the twentieth century, and remembered for his wealth and lavish lifestyle, he died at only 58 and – to judge from what he said to Michael Parkinson – he would no doubt be the first person to admit that his somewhat premature death was a sort of suicide. This despite the fact that it was neither cigarettes nor alcohol that caused it, but a cerebral hemorrhage.

Richard Burton was a man of high intelligence as well as an exceptionally gifted actor and, despite his problems of living both with himself and with any woman that he loved, he had clear insight *and* a great love for the world. He told Parkinson that a characteristic of the Welsh was to get close to the precipice and, when asked about his own experience of pulling himself back from the brink, he replied (I think rather oddly), 'I did suddenly wake up one morning and found how splendidly rich and extraordinary the world was, and then I couldn't bear its richness and its beauty. And in order to obviate the idea of the richness and extraordinary beauty of the world, I thought it best to leave it.' He stated emphatically that he would never think of taking his own life by taking an overdose or anything similar, but admitted that he had been drinking himself to death.

'Money is the root of all evil' may well be a cliché, but there is nevertheless a great deal of truth in it. Talking of his 30 years of living in Hollywood, Richard Burton was, again, completely clear-sighted, open and frank. He said that it was a very pleasant place, full of people who were nice as well as rich, but that it had 'no root'. And talking of the famous present that he gave to Elizabeth Taylor, he said, 'When I heard that it was the world's most expensive diamond, I just *had* to have it... I don't know why I got it.' He admitted that it was unusual for someone from his humble background to have the opportunity of so many temptations, but obviously thought it completely natural to succumb to them. Well, he is undoubtedly right, since desire is one of the most common of human failings. It is in fact nothing to be ashamed of – most us would die if we felt no desire for food or drink – but spiritual understanding teaches us that while we are down here we need to learn not to let desires dominate us. Sathya Sai Baba instigated a 'Ceiling on Desires' program. This is not to say that we should not enjoy the many things that our world has to offer us, but moderation and sharing clearly make for greater happiness all round.

Raju – one of the many spirits I have met who also succumbed to worldly temptations – was a rather dishonest Indian who ran a coconut stall and did not want to leave because he was making quite a lot of money from overcharging innumerate people. Once I had discussed with him the full implications of his way of life, he became able to see things from the point of view of the people he had been cheating. I was then able to persuade him that it might now be time to broaden his horizons, and so he called for his deceased grandmother to escort him to the other side.

When I was working with tsunami victims, I encountered an American family who were having their 'vacation of a lifetime' and did not want it to end. Interestingly, the daughter (Alison), who was only about 4 years old, understood what had happened and tried to lead them on, but they refused to leave their holiday resort. However, when I told them that they could return to Earth once they had done some more learning on the other side, they were quite willing to follow the wise young Alison.

On a completely different continent, Patrick was a racist Australian who had killed many Aborigines and wanted to continue doing so until all the indigenous people of his country had been wiped out. It was not easy to get him to repent, but we were shown a life in which Patrick had been black himself and this made him realize his mistake. He then called for one of his victims, who was willing to accept Patrick's apology before leading him across to the other side.

Another very different sort of case was that of Peter and Maggie, a middle-aged couple who weren't so much *attached* to worldly pursuits but so embroiled in day-to-day life as to be unable to escape from it. They were arguing over whose turn it was to do the washing up, and by that I do not mean, 'Let me do it, dear, because you did it yesterday', but more like, 'I'm always doing it and you hardly ever do'! Once I had given them the good news that neither needed to do it any more, I got them to change their bodies to what they had been like when they first fell in love. This helped them to appreciate their folly and to be able to call for their parents.

Frank, on the other hand, was a jolly man who was not alcoholic but simply did not want to leave the pub in Ludlow because drinking with his mates was the only thing he really enjoyed. Judging by his style of dress he had obviously been there for a good couple of centuries at least and, when pushed hard, he did admit to occasional boredom. He completely lacked any spirit of adventure and so no sort of travel had any appeal to him. However, when I mentioned the word 'women', that did strike a chord from Frank's early life, even though he had long since given up on them. He then remembered a young girl named Sophia that he had once been very attracted to. Frank still had no appeal to Sophia, but she was nevertheless perfectly willing to lead him across to look for other girls.

Gallows are one thing that we in Britain are happy to have seen the last of many years ago. Another is the 'ducking stool', which was a fairly common form of punishment, at least in towns which had a river or a pond. Evidently this was used in Ripon, in North Yorkshire, and there I once met Stephen, who had got to so enjoy being in charge of the ducking stool that he was still torturing people in this way several centuries on! I had to convince him not only that the people he thought he was ducking did not really exist, but also that there were much more worthwhile things to do and that being kind to people brings much greater happiness. Naturally it turned out that Stephen himself had never experienced kindness during his lifetime, but I nevertheless got him to call for his grandfather, who had treated him a little better than his parents had.

On the other side of the world I once came across three men in Machu Picchu who wanted to get their hands on all the money that was coming in from the tourists. After pointing out to them that they were not having any success, I managed to persuade them that they would have no use for it anyway! Fortunately they each had a parent or grandparent to call for.

Back in England was Valerie, a prostitute who had never learned anything about love, but nevertheless did not want to give up her way of life – the only thing she knew. When I suggested that it would be to her advantage to find someone who would love her as the real Valerie rather than a mere sex object, she found it hard to understand the point I was making. So I told her that she could learn about such things as real love if she crossed over, and she then called for the previous manager of the whorehouse in which she had been employed, who appeared to have learned a lot since she died.

The Ludlow Conservative Party headquarters are in what is frequently described as 'England's most beautiful street' (Broad Street), and there I met Piers, a fat, balding man, who had been a member of the Party and was still attached to his good-quality food and drink. He was not very easy to deal with, but I did persuade him to call for his grandfather. The same was true of Hugh, a fat old man who really enjoyed his roast beef in The Blue Boar (in Mill Street, Ludlow, which runs parallel to Broad Street). In this case I did succeed in persuading him to be more adventurous, and his father came readily when called.

I don't know about you, but there is hardly anything that annoys me more than people who create scams or spread viruses on the internet. Recently (inspired by a book I had heard about[3] which amusingly relayed all the email conversations that the author had had with a number of these 'scammers' – if that is a word) I decided to challenge someone who called himself the Reverend Dan Amigo, and who claimed that he wanted to give me 12.8 million dollars. It occurred to me when I received his first email that the person who had sent it must be a 'real human being with an immortal soul' and so, since I was keen to find out something about him, we corresponded for about four months. Though he learned quite a lot about me, I failed miserably both in getting to know him and in convincing him of the futility of what he was doing. The money was allegedly sitting in a Nigerian bank because its owner had died with nobody to inherit it, and Dan claimed to be a banker as well as a Catholic priest. When I refused to give him my bank details, he urged me to meet him either in Ghana or Madrid 'to arrange the transfer', but would never give me more than his word to prove the existence of the money. He further had no reply to my list of eight reasons why I refused to believe that he was a priest. (These included his total inability to quote the first six words of St. John's Gospel!) Despite my protests that the money should not leave Africa, where the need is much greater, he said that it was being shipped to Spain (in boxes!). Although I was intrigued to know what would have happened either if I had flown off somewhere to meet him or if I had taken up his suggestion of opening a brand new account for receiving the money, I refrained from both – especially since I was told that I would have to pay my own fare to either Ghana or Madrid. He ceased replying to my emails only after I had explained to him three times exactly which worthy causes I wished the cash to be distributed to.

This of course is by the way, but during the course of the correspondence I met a group of six Nigerian men who were trying to 'help' poor people in their country by this sort of fraudulent means. They had all been killed in a truck crash together because one of them was driving too fast. After giving them a bit of a lecture about how they were messing people up and not getting any benefit even for themselves by what they were doing on the internet, I succeeded in convincing them that they were dead by getting one of them to imagine that he was 6 years old again. When they all saw how this man's body changed, they believed me, and I hope they also believed me when I told them there were much more worthwhile things to do. Anyway, they all thought of someone to call for.

When I first started doing psychopomp work I never expected to come across animals who were stuck, but this has happened on various occasions. One was a fox, who was thoroughly enjoying himself killing thought-form chickens after imagining that he had escaped from the hunters. After convincing him that he had in fact lost his life, I persuaded him to go somewhere where everyone was friends and there was no killing, and he called for his foxy father.

Although I introduced this section on attachment by mentioning Richard Burton because his life interests me, he is not in actual fact a good example of someone who failed to cross over on account of his attachments to worldly pursuits or his addiction to alchohol. (Or cigarettes, for that matter, despite the fact that throughout the Parkinson interview he was lighting up one cigarette after another!) It is my belief that neither Richard Burton nor Elizabeth Taylor became irrevocably ensnared by the wealth that their success brought – Taylor in particular became much involved in good works towards the end of her life – and, when I asked on one of my journeys about his and Elizabeth's fate, the answer I got was that, after his death, free from the lures of alcohol, cigarettes or diamonds, Richard had hung around waiting for her and that, once she had died too, they were straight away able to cross over together. However, as my above-mentioned cases have shown, many people are alas unable to see beyond the attractions of materialism, and these continue to pursue them after death.

7. Attachment to a person

Since we are all interdependent, it is at least as natural to become over-attached to another human being as it is to be reluctant to abandon worldly pursuits. Following on from Richard Burton and Elizabeth Taylor, there can be few people who are not familiar with the song 'Some Enchanted Evening' from Richard Rodgers' musical *South Pacific*. It continues:

You may see a stranger across a crowded room,
And somehow you know, you know even then
That somewhere you'll see her again and again.
Who can explain it? Who can tell you why?
Fools give you reasons; wise men never try.

Well, I am afraid that in my second book[1] I joined the fools! I explained that the 'instant recognition' sometimes felt on a first meeting was due to soul-mate or twin-soul connections. The links between twin souls are particularly strong since they are literally two halves of a whole, and I explained how, since the link is so very strong, it can be an extraordinarily powerful cause of pain. I have met one or two examples of this in my rescue work. Martin, for instance, had got into such a violent argument with Geraldine, his twin soul, that he had actually thrown her under a train! As a result he was so consumed with guilt and grief that he had killed himself. Getting him to forgive himself took a bit of doing, but Geraldine was more than ready to come and collect him.

Another twin-soul couple were Theo and Rose. Theo died first and, not being a believer, he thought that he would cease to exist once his body had been consumed. What I saw initially was a man's body covered in worms, with a woman crouching over it.

So I brushed all the worms off and then showed Theo that he still had a wonderful body. Rose may well have taken to heart the line in the above song: 'Once you have found her (in this case "him"), never let her go'! She had failed to cross over because of her concern for Theo and her desire to be with him, but it had not been possible for her to help him unaided. Once Theo was convinced that it was only his physical body that had died, he was able to recognize Rose. Then he called for his grandfather and they went happily off with him together.

Dorothy and Sidney's twin-soul bond was of a very different nature because Dorothy was a real pain in the neck and, although they were married, he had never loved her. (Sometimes, when people are less evolved, it is only one party who recognizes the twin-soul bond.) When Sid died, Dorothy hung on to him and, on account of the bond between them being so strong, this prevented him from crossing over. I explained the situation to him, assuring him that he would come to really love her once she had worked out her present problems and become less selfish, and then I suggested that he could cut the ties between them. He saw that these were at the solar plexus (the seat of power), as well as the hands and feet, and cutting them all gave him a wonderful feeling of liberation. He then called for his father. (In cases of twin-soul relationships the ties can never be cut permanently, but temporary severing can on occasion be helpful for both parties.)

Emily and her lover Roland were not as far as I know twin souls, but she could nevertheless not bear the idea of leaving the house in Mill Street, Ludlow, where Roland had lived. I convinced her that he was no longer there by showing her that the house was now a pottery shop. She then called for her great-uncle, who was able to take her to Roland.

Mavis was attached to her son Joel for a very different reason. He had locked her up in a garret and so in revenge she was haunting him. She had stayed in the garret until Joel's death, and then she had left the house and followed him to the graveyard at the bottom of Corve Street in Ludlow, where she remained until I met her. She needed some therapy for her traumatic experience but, once she was ready for reconciliation, she was able to call for Joel, who was fortunately now repentant and able to help her across.

Hubert in Shrewsbury, on the other hand, had been a jealous husband to Julia, always nagged her and never trusted her fidelity. After his death the relieved Julia had felt free to remarry, but the new husband was so troubled by Hubert haunting the house that he had not stayed. She eventually died too of course, but not before having had a series of male partners with whom the same thing always happened. Hubert did not know that Julia had died and so, as happens most frequently, I had to convince him by pointing out the changes that had taken place in Shrewsbury. She came a trifle reluctantly when called and was somewhat relieved to be informed that he could no longer trouble her and would have a karmic debt to pay her. I left the two of them to work out a reconciliation on the other side, and

Hubert followed Julia quite meekly.

Syria has of course had many much more recent deaths. Just after one of the worst bombing incidents in Homs, I came across a mother who had been killed together with her small daughter. She was stuck firstly because of being upset about her little one's life being 'wasted', and secondly because she was so worried about how her husband would cope without her. This case could of course also be included in the section entitled 'Responsibility'. And the young child was stuck too on account of ignorance as to what had happened.

Jack and Terry were in The Unicorn, one of Ludlow's historic pubs, arguing over Nelly, their shared mistress (who was the twin soul of neither). The silly thing was that neither of them wanted her full time anyway, since neither had any intention of leaving his somewhat unsatisfactory marriage. Asked how much they really loved her, they admitted that it was more a case of sexual gratification than true love and, once I had convinced them that Nelly was no longer alive either, they each agreed to call for a parent. (In this case it would of course have been possible to get them to call for Nelly, but I was afraid that this would simply prolong the argument!)

Linda was a Western girl who was on honeymoon in Thailand when the 2006 tsunami struck. Duncan, her husband, had not died and she could not bear to leave him. I told her that they could marry again in a future life, that she would meet many more friends on the other side, and that Duncan, who was destined to live longer, would also meet other people who could be important to him. This persuaded her to call for her grandmother.

Jason was a zookeeper in Chester, who had been mauled by a lion. He was hanging on on the Earth plane not because of attachment to a person, but on account of his love for the lions. So I told him that he could have a lion as his totem animal, and also suggested that he might, for instance, like to work in a game park in Africa in his next life. This persuaded him to leave and he called for his father.

Martin was another man who was attached to animals. In this case it was bears of whom he was a keeper, and he could not bear (no pun intended!) to leave them since he regarded them as his only friends. So, rather than asking him to call for a person, I got him to call for one of his deceased bears.

Attachment, however, can work both ways. In Jennifer's case it was her husband who would not let either her or their cat go after they had died. I helped her by cutting the ties to him, but she was then a bit apprehensive about calling for her mother, who had not liked cats. I assured her that her mother would have changed in the spirit world, and the mother, when she came, obligingly proved this by giving them both a welcoming embrace.

8. Attachment to alcohol (or drugs, cigarettes, etc.)

I am not going to attempt to answer the question 'What was it that drove Richard Burton to alcoholism?', partly because I do not know enough about what went on in his mind, partly because I am no expert on the causes of alcoholism, and – even more – because individual cases are not of great relevance to this particular book. What concern me more here are the general problems that can prevent people from leaving the Earth's plane after they have died. When Michael Parkinson interviewed Richard Burton, he had recently come out from a Catholic hospital in Santa Monica to which he had been admitted for drying out. His case had been very serious indeed, since his consumption of hard liquor had risen to between two and three bottles a day, and his doctor had given him two weeks to live. It was the notion of 'two weeks' and the number of seconds, hours and days that made up such a period that made him quite literally, in his own words, 'pull back from the brink'. He said,

'I've been there and I've seen that dark wood and I know how terrible it is, how frightening it is …' But for many people the cause and effects of alcoholism are quite different. Most succumb to it not through any desire to escape from the 'beauty' of the world, as Burton did, but rather on the contrary because they are failing completely to see any beauty anywhere in life, have sunk into depression, and want to blot out their sorrows. They, unlike Burton, fail to pull back from the brink just in time and consequently remain trapped in their addiction. The result of this is that their spirits tend to attach themselves to incarnate alcoholics or to hang around public houses, where they can continue drinking vicariously. But of course doing anything vicariously never brings satisfaction, and so their problems can never be solved until they have been released from the Earth's plane.

In July 2004 (one month before our move to Ludlow and four months before the Simon Buxton workshop that got me started on this work) I went to Scotland for an 'ancestralization' organized by Jed Pemberton under the slightly detached supervision of Malidoma Somé. (Malidoma wanted to remain in the background as he felt it important that we Europeans develop our own ways of doing things.) In Africa it is the custom when anyone dies to perform a ritual in which the person's soul is directed to the world of spirit, but since, as Malidoma explains in his autobiographical book,[4] this has for a long time now not been practiced in the West, we have a lot of catching up to do. The weekend was particularly interesting on account of being the first of its kind, but it can also be said that it was experimental. Each of us was asked to select just two of our own deceased ancestors – one of each sex – and the idea was that those selected would gather up all the other members of the family and escort them over 'en bloc'.

Well, on the very first psychopomp journey that I did on my own at home, one of the people I met was my uncle John, who had been an alcoholic. He was hanging around London trying to benefit from the drinks that incarnate Londoners were enjoying. After greeting him I asked whether he had been involved in the ceremony that had taken place in Scotland, and he replied rather grumpily, 'No one told me about it!' This made perfect sense to me since the poor man had been regarded as something of a black sheep in my family. (After he had failed to take my father's advice to join Alcoholics Anonymous, my father had banned him from our home, and so my poor mother, who was always very loving and loyal to everyone in her family, had had to visit him on her own whenever she was able to get herself to London.) He was obviously still feeling like an outcast and this was clearly preventing him from moving on, but I assured him that my grandmother, who had been just as saintly as my mother, still loved him. So, with some trepidation, he called for his mother and was forgiven, which was lovely to behold. Then he moved happily to the light.

Ludlow, like most English towns, has many public houses and many of these are very old. I once encountered Ernest, Luke,

Willy and Ralph merrily drinking ale together in a pub in Quality Square in the most historic part of Ludlow. There were also other men drinking there, who were so engrossed in their own world that they completely ignored me, but the four I mention were fortunately ready to listen. Willy had lost a daughter and was drinking to drown his sorrows, Luke was grieving the loss of his son, while Ernest and Ralph were simply drinking out of habit, but all four were open to being led out of the little square to the market, where I pointed out to them the changes that had occurred since they had last observed it. This convinced them that it was time to move on. Willy's daughter and Luke's son came to collect them immediately when called, and Ernest called for his mother and Ralph his father.

Immediately after I had rescued Ollie, the tramp mentioned above, who had died of hypothermia, I met his alcoholic mother, Sheila, who was also still Earthbound. This was before I had got into the habit of asking the lost souls their names, yet, when she said, 'Fred?', it did not feel right to me. So then she said, 'Oh, you must mean Ollie. He's no good!' I did not want to go deeply into the facts of how she herself had contributed to Ollie turning out the way he had – that could be dealt with on the other side – but I did get her to agree with me that it would be much better not to be dependent upon drink. When we had finished our conversation, she called for the man she had always loved, who was not Ollie's father. He came and was happy to lead her away, despite obviously not requiting her feelings.

Brother Matthew was an alcoholic monk who had crept into a pub in Ludlow's Quality Square in order to continue drinking vicariously. I persuaded him that on the other side there were nicer-tasting drinks than the poor quality ale that was being served there in his day (I must mention, though, that local ale is excellent nowadays!), and he then called for the senior monk who had tried to help him overcome his addiction.

Jimmy, Tom, Johnnie, Tim and Paddy were having a drunken

brawl in the upper floor of Ludlow's very popular Church Inn. It was a habit they had had for a long time and did not know how to get out of. Being taken outside into the street and shown how the town had moved on since they were alive convinced them of the need to do something different, and they each had a deceased relative to call upon.

I found Bryn, an elderly Welsh drunkard, drifting down the river into which he had fallen. His wife had left him because of the drink, his children would no longer speak to him either, and he had absolutely nothing to live for. Since, however, he still had fond memories of his mother, who had died when he was only 10, he was happy to call for her.

Josh had been killed in a car crash on account of his addiction to drink. I met him on his way to the pub and managed to dissuade him to continue on the journey on account of the fact that it could be harmful to another person besides himself if he became a 'spirit attachment'. When he called for his grandfather, it turned out that he had always worried about Josh's grandmother, who had also been an alcoholic. I did not find out what had happened to her, but this is an example of how such things as alcoholism often run in families.

There are of course other addictions besides alcohol. Chris was a drug dealer in New York, who had become fed up with the ring of 12 other men who were also dealers and depended on him for their supplies. I am not sure whether it was drugs that had killed all of them, but I did succeed in convincing Chris that he was free to escape from it all now that he was dead. I also spoke to a couple of the others. Robin was 52 and overweight and so, when I asked him to think about what he had looked like 30 years previously, he was amazed to see his 22-year-old, handsome body. Clinton, who changed himself into a 25-year-old, told me that he had not got into drugs until he was older than that and agreed with me that it was better not to be dependent on them. Seeing the changes in Robin and Clinton convinced all 13 men that they were dead, and they all thought of someone to call for.

Someone else who had got into drugs (I think in the 1960s) was a young girl named Dolly. She had been to the same secondary school as myself (Clifton High School for Girls in Bristol), though I am not aware that we knew each other. This school is situated on the same street as Clifton College, the prestigious boys' public school, and in my day the girls were not permitted to walk down College Road, nor the boys up it! Dolly, whose parents were extremely strict, railed against this and, being also consumed with curiosity about the boys, she took to secretly walking down there out of school hours. She even found a way of repeatedly getting into the college grounds, where she made friends with Pete and Mike, who made a regular habit of having a secret smoke. She prided herself on never being found out and, when she was 16, she left school and followed her friends to Manchester, delighted to escape from home. The two boys were a couple of years older than she was and both went to Manchester University, while she did a secretarial course. She had sex with both of them while still at school and imagined that she would in due course marry one or other of them, but there were no real feelings on either side and, once at Manchester, the lads made other friends. Dolly got into another crowd and was gradually led on from cigarettes to drugs. She seduced many of the young men she met, one of whom, Barry, died from an overdose. This shook Dolly up a great deal, but not enough to make her give up the drugs herself. After herself dying from an overdose, all she could think of doing was to carry on hanging around with people who were still taking drugs. Once I had persuaded her that she could escape to something better, she called for Barry.

Drug addiction is one of the most serious problems of our day, and one to which there alas seems to be no obvious solution. However, when we remember that the purpose of being on Earth is to learn, we must remain hopeful about everyone learning their lessons eventually.

9. Attachment to property

Old properties are renowned for being haunted, and it seems sad that not everyone yet appreciates that this is something that can easily be remedied. *All* the residents – both past and present – can clearly be happier when those who no longer belong there have moved on! Ludlow's very attractive Broad Street (said to be the most beautiful street in England) has a most interesting house which goes right across it at the bottom, part of which is attached to some of the remains of the old city wall. The middle part of Broadgate House has no ground floor, but instead an arch through which traffic can pass and join Lower Broad Street. Well, the elderly Herman – not surprisingly – was extremely attached to this exceptional property, which he had been very proud to own, and was angry both about the fact that there were other people now living there and about the noise made by the cars going underneath 'his' living room. When I had told him that, if he crossed over, he could acquire an equally nice house with no traffic, he was willing to call for his father.

In March 2012 my husband and I went on a U3A (University of the Third Age) trip to Wales, where we visited a fascinating old manor house named Llancaiach. The guides (I mean incarnate ones!) there dress in seventeenth-century costumes and talk to the visitors in English of the period, which we found to be great fun. While we were looking at the exhibition prior to being given our tour of the house, I noticed that various hauntings of the house were listed. Wanting to keep an open mind, I did not write these down or commit them to memory, but on my next journey, just a couple of days later, I asked to be taken to Llancaiach. After dispatching 20 men who were still worrying about the English Civil War and busy with the juridical court in the Great Hall, I came across Anna, the dairy maid, upstairs in the attic (where most of the 30 servants had slept). She was very upset both about the disappearance of the cows and about the fact that the owner of the manor, Mr. Pritchard (whom she knew to be dead), had no surviving son to succeed him. She herself had no family and had never had any home of her own other than the manor, and so was extremely reluctant to leave it. She was consequently hanging on there in the hope that one of the daughters, Jane or Mary, would have a son, who would then come and reclaim the house for the family. The fact that there were people around wearing the costumes and speaking the language with which she was familiar made it more difficult for Anna to appreciate that we were now in the twenty-first century. I had to point out to her the new part of the premises, which now holds the restaurant for the many visitors, and the cars and coaches, but once I had got through to her, she was able to call for Mr. Pritchard. (I would normally suggest calling for someone closer to the person concerned than he was, but Anna had no family or friends to call for.)

My dear old cousin Phoebe was another person who apparently slipped through the net at the ancestralization weekend in Scotland that I mentioned above. She, who remained single all her life, was my grandfather's first cousin and she inherited the family home in North Oxford following the death of my great-aunt Judith Anne (after whom I was named). Phoebe's was a sad life because she had been one of the first women to go to Oxford University, but a nervous breakdown had prevented her from ever making any real use of her Classical studies. Her Park Town house (in which I myself lived with my parents and two younger siblings during World War Two) was close to her college, Lady Margaret Hall, and when she died she left the house to my parents. Phoebe never worked – there was enough family money for her to live on – and I am not aware that she had any friends. She used to love it when I was working in London and invited myself for the weekend (especially since she had never learned to cook and so could ask me to do 'exciting' dishes such as fish fingers and peas!), and apart from that my only memories of her are firstly her rigidity and secondly the fact that she was afflicted by Parkinson's disease. Included in the rigidity were inflexible meal times, which meant that if one had the misfortune to have been kept late at work and miss a train, there would be no chance of any food being offered upon one's arrival.

So again it was no big surprise to me to find that Cousin Phoebe had not heard about the Merivale-Cazabon family ancestralization either. I found her sitting on an island waiting for a boat to take her back to Oxford. She seemed to know vaguely at least that she was dead because she recognized that the Park Town house was no longer hers, but she told me that she wanted to 'live there with Stephen and Norah' (my parents). I started explaining the situation to her, but before I had finished my father turned up and told Cousin Phoebe himself that he and my mother were both dead too. Then the two of us took her to Oxford together (I demonstrated how it could be done without bothering with a boat!), so that she could see for herself that the Park Town house was now occupied by other people. She still failed to be happy about things, but recognized that there could be no benefit from hanging around. When I asked her to call for someone she cared about who was dead, she called for her mother, who promptly escorted her to the light.

But, human nature being what it is, it is not only very old properties that can be haunted. Lee and Carlo were two brothers who had lived with their mother in one of the areas of the United States that were badly hit by the 2011 tornadoes. The house was completely destroyed and, since they knew that their mother was dead, they were arguing about their inheritance! I explained gently that, if they called for their mother, she could explain what she had really meant to say in her will, and also that they no longer actually needed the inheritance. They took a bit of convincing, but the mother soon took over from me and led them away.

Also killed by one of these terrible tornadoes were Jessie and Georgina, two black women who lived in identical houses. They were arguing over whose was the house that had not been completely destroyed. I suggested that generous hospitality would be in order here and also told them that, if they crossed over, they could each build themselves a new, even better, house. This assurance enabled them each to call for a grandparent.

More recently there have been yet more of these fearsome weather conditions, and in March 2012 I went to Louisiana and talked to a poor, black family who were very upset about their house having been destroyed by the hurricane. Ned and Nell introduced me to their children, Jasmine and Jake, and then talked about how long and hard they had had to work and save in order to buy their house. It was easy to understand why they were so upset and, after offering my condolences, I explained to them that, if they crossed over, they would be able to build a stronger house for free. That made them decide to call for Nell's mother.

Kevin and Janet were a married couple who lived near Cardiff and were constantly having rows with each other. Their current argument was that Janet said that Kevin was overfeeding the cat. One thing that annoyed them even more than each other, however, were the new occupants of 'their' house, who they complained were 'in their way'. So I had to inform them that in fact it was the other way round! They were not easily convinced, but eventually agreed to call for one of their parents.

Walter was a captain, who was still attached not to his house but to his ship, and he had no desire to relinquish command of it. However, once I had made him appreciate that his life and duties were now over, he also proved willing to call for his father.

10. Anger and desire for revenge

Anger is one of the most common of human emotions while we are on Earth, and also one of the most damaging. After death it may no longer be able to cause illness but, like other negative emotions, it can easily prevent a soul from being ready and willing to cross over. Next door to the house in Ludlow's Mill Street which is now a pottery shop was a widow named Maud, who was completely stuck in her anger about her husband having been killed in battle. She had surrounded herself by a black wall, which I had to dissolve by blowing light onto it, and once that had been done and I had pointed out to her that her anger had caused her to be stuck in a dark place for an unnecessarily long time, she found herself able to call for Richard, her husband.

Also in Ludlow I met Polly, who had been so mistreated as a child that she had become a 'witch' with the aim of getting her own back on absolutely everybody. I discussed with her the reasons why it was better to forgive people and learn to love, and eventually, since there had never been anyone at all who had shown her any love, she remembered a woman who had been a great benefactor in the town and became able to call for her.

Tony's was a milder case of anger and had been caused by the new supermarket building that was completed in Ludlow before we moved here (but not at all long ago in the framework of such a historic town). We have learned that there was a great deal of controversy over the building of Ludlow's Tesco, and so I was not particularly surprised when the very young Tony told me that he was cross about the loss of his playground. So I explained to him that he would be able to find even better playgrounds on the other side, and then he called happily for the grandfather about whose death he had been sad.

A very different sort of case was that of Wayne, an American basketball player who had been injured in play and consequently failed to make it into the NBA. He was unable to move on on account of being trapped in bitterness, but I convinced him that he could eventually get another chance in a new body if he crossed over. He also then called for his grandfather.

Hassan was killed in the terrible Egyptian football riot of 2011 and was stuck in Egypt because of his anger about it. (He differed from the dozen men I mentioned above who were ignorant as to what had happened.) Once I had succeeded in persuading him that hanging on to anger could only hurt him even more, he called for his grandfather.

On my astral visit to Syria just after one of the bad bombings in Homs, I came across a group of six men who were stuck in their anger with President Assad and were clinging on because of having a huge desire for revenge. I told them that I sympathized with their feelings, but that being unforgiving could not help anyone, and that Assad would undoubtedly be forced to depart in due course. I further pointed out that if they crossed over, they would be in a much better position to help their country, and they were then all persuaded to call for a relative.

At the end of 2010 my husband and I visited Australia, where we were welcomed by my Australian cousin, who lives in Canberra. On a journey after our return home, I met an Aboriginal chief who I think had been dead for quite a long time, but who was (understandably!) still angry about what the white settlers had done in his country. I told him that I sympathized, but that there had been big improvements in recent years, and to prove it I took him to Canberra and showed him the wonderful Australian National Museum, which displays Aboriginal art and other things in such an appreciative manner. I also told him that he could do more to combat racism from the other side and that he could then return to Earth to do more work in this field – 'even as a white person' – to which he replied, 'Heaven forbid!' He got the message, however, and was then happy to call for his esteemed grandfather.

Another man whom I found to be justifiably angry was an American Indian (I'll call him Red Feather), whose land had been taken and who was wanting to take vengeance on white people for killing his son. When I suggested that his people were normally peaceable and forgiving, he replied, 'To Hell with that!' Then I told him that many Americans felt quite differently now and were trying to make up for the past. To prove it I took him to see the wonderful American Indian Museum in New York. Then Red Feather called for his son, who proved to be not vengeful at all and told his father that he had volunteered for a short life. So eventually Red Feather was happy to be led across by his son.

In the summer of 2011 there were riots, arson, looting and even a few fatal accidents in several of Britain's major cities. All this was triggered initially by a shooting by police, but was fueled by the anger that many people felt over issues such as unemployment and social injustice. When I met Spencer in Birmingham, he was still so angry about what had been happening and his own 'lousy life' that he did not want to tell me his name at first. Once I had succeeded in calming him down a bit, he remembered a deceased teacher whom he had admired when he was at school and called for him.

Early in 2012 BBC Television showed a series about some of the world's most dangerous roads. One of these concerned the highway built in Alaska for the sole purpose of developing and managing the oil industry there. I was intrigued by the program, despite the fact that it seemed to me sheer madness for an Englishman and his inexperienced female companion to attempt such a drive. They survived of course – otherwise the broadcast would not have gone ahead – but only at considerable (and in my opinion quite unnecessary!) risk to their lives. Without having seen this episode of the series I would have remained ignorant of this road's existence, and only a few days later my psychopomp journey took me to Alaska, where I found a certain man named Jerry very angry about his death. His job had been as a driver of one of the massive trucks that haul materials to and from the oil station and, more often than not, he made the journey jointly with his mate Ben. (People often jokingly used to ask them for an ice-cream!) These trucks are so heavy, and the icy conditions on this road are often so bad, that it is impossible for the drivers to brake and stop, so it is no wonder that there have been quite a few fatalities. When Ben and Jerry's truck had got into difficulties and they had had to pull off the road, Jerry had suffered a lower back injury and then died of hypothermia before it was possible for a rescue team to reach them. Ben, however, had survived, and this was what was making Jerry angry and resentful. Once I had calmed him down and told him that, when he returned to Earth next time, he could do a less dangerous job, he called for his friend Trip, who had been killed in an earlier accident on the same route.

11. Mental illness

Mental illness is a very sad thing in any circumstances and, as with many other things, death does not bring an instant cure to it. In fact it can be a contributory factor in preventing someone from appreciating that they have died. When I lived in the Hull area in northern England, I did my best to befriend a woman in my parish who had had an appalling childhood and a very unhappy life ever since, and whose mental stability deteriorated over the years during which I knew her. She ended her days in a psychiatric hospital and it therefore did not surprise me to meet her on one of my journeys. She told me pathetically that she felt desperately alone and that neither Father Storey (the parish priest who had always been very good to her) nor Jean (a neighbor who had also done a lot for her and visited regularly) was around. When I explained the situation to her and told her that Father Storey had also himself recently died, she called for him to take her across.

Another woman, Brenda, was to be found in a psychiatric hospital in Sydney, Australia. She was a rather pathetic old woman who had never been cared about and had no idea that there was any escape from her situation. When I told her that *I* cared about her, she was skeptical and wanted to know who I was. After telling her a little bit about myself, I got her to think back to her youth and, when she did this, I was able to make her appreciate how her body had changed – proof that change was possible. She then told me that Grandma Smith, who died when Brenda was only 10, had cared about her, and Grandma Smith of course came immediately when called.

On another occasion I came across a young man named Ian who had 'lost his mind' and fallen in love with a mermaid. I had to convince him not only that he was dead, but also that the mermaid he kept trying to catch was only a thought form that he had himself created and that mermaids were purely mythical. Once I had succeeded in doing this, he called for his deceased mother.

Alec, whose mother had died when he was a child, had also 'lost his mind' and thought that birds were his only friends. I met him completely surrounded by blue tits, and explaining things to him was a little bit difficult, but when I reminded him about his deceased mother, who had loved him, he remembered enough to be able to call for her.

Daphne's was a similar story. At first I saw only butterflies, but then the young girl appeared, and it seemed that since 'losing her mind' chasing butterflies was her only pleasure. Her mother had died when she was tiny and so, after we had talked a little and I had shown her how the butterflies were mere thought forms, Daphne willingly called for her mother.

Vincent, on the other hand, was a young lad who had not so much 'lost his mind', but rather had been born a 'simpleton' (for want of a better word). He had fallen into a well when trying to catch his reflection and was unable to get out. I got hold of a rope to pull him out and then got him to call for his mother, who had died when he was a baby.

The main building of Bristol University, where I did my degree, has a tall tower, and the city also has a well-known suspension bridge, which crosses the River Avon. When I met Justin, a Bristol graduate, he told me that he had seriously considered throwing himself off both of these, but had funked it each time. His sad story was that his parents, who were not graduates, had put a great deal of pressure on him to succeed and – probably as a result of their excessive expectations – he had never done as well as he thought he should have done in examinations and felt ashamed about it. He had ended up with a third-class degree and then drifted from one unsatisfactory job to another, never finding fulfillment in anything. He had married an insecure girl, who also put continual pressure on him to get a better job, and became increasingly unstable mentally until he was eventually taken into a psychiatric hospital. However, he kept escaping and wandering off, and it was on one of his sorties that he lost his life. Whether that was from hypothermia, under-nourishment or something else was unclear, but it was quite clear that he was completely lost. When I assured him that he could, with help, get to a better place, he called for 'Grandfather Gerald', who had been good to him when he was very young.

On a recent journey I spent the whole half-hour in the south of France. After dealing with 22 people in Nice who thought that they had found paradise there, I went to the hospital of St. Rémy near Arles, renowned for its famous one-time inhabitant Vincent van Gogh. There I met, among others, Pierre, a man with absolutely no sense of self-worth, who kept beating himself 'to death', but did not believe that he had died because everything was 'still exactly the same'. I asked whether he had known van Gogh and he replied in the affirmative. He could not, however, believe that Vincent had become famous until I took him out into the garden of the hospital and showed him the reproductions of the wonderful paintings now exhibited there (the originals being of course scattered throughout art galleries in various different parts of the world). Never having known anyone who cared about him, Pierre consequently called for the great man himself (who arrived, I am glad to say, with his ear restored to the side of his head!).

Alzheimer's and dementia are both a very sad, and alas a very common, fate among people in our society, but one of the least recognized problems about them is that they can prevent people from having a conscious death. One such case was that of an elderly Swiss man named Johann, whom I met wandering around Zermatt with his dog, Karl. I blew away the thought-form dog so that Johann could see that he was not living in reality and then explained to him that he and Karl were both dead, but that Karl's spirit would come to him when called. This delighted him, and he then also called for his mother to lead them away.

12. Feeling unworthy

Feelings of unworthiness are a most common affliction among those who are given insufficient love, and the Churches also have a great deal to answer for with the threat of eternal damnation perpetrated over so many years. We know only too well that in the past it was very easy for a woman – particularly if she had healing powers – to be labeled as a 'wicked witch'. Most of these so-called 'witches' knew that they were only working for the good of others, but poor Ariadne's mother had convinced her from an early age that she really was evil. When I met her she was busy stirring a brew that she had concocted, and I had to talk her out of the 'wicked witch' role that had been hers for so long. It turned out that her father, who had died when she was very small, had loved her, and remembering that love enabled Ariadne to call for him.

I think the Church can also be blamed for the plight of a certain 'Jonah'. This was not the man's real name, but he saw himself as a sort of Jonah. He had in fact been eaten by sharks rather than swallowed by a whale, but he had during his last life on Earth been so brainwashed by priests about the horrors of Hell that he decided that he was safe inside the 'whale' and that it was certainly preferable to Hell. So I suggested that he call for someone who he was quite sure *was* good enough for Heaven and he called for his mother.

A very different sort of case was that of Hank, a dwarf who had been regarded as 'only good for the circus', but had then failed even at that. He got shown a picture of himself in a previous life in which he had been a big strong man who had despised anyone who was physically deformed, especially dwarves. This made him realize that there had been karmic reasons for his having been a dwarf that time round, which in turn made it easier for him to accept his plight. He then appreciated that he had now learned his lesson and that it was consequently now time to move on. Since no one had ever given him any love, he called for Edward, a 'dwarf king' whom he had admired.

Toby was another dwarf, and he was hiding in the kitchen in

Ludlow's most famous hotel, The Feathers. He had worked there and did not want to leave after his death because he was so ashamed of his size. So I showed him how he could now change his body by simply thinking of how he would like to look, and that gave him the courage to call for his deceased grandmother.

A couple of weeks after the Boxing Day tsunami, I was called to a fire that had been lit for burning bodies, but had got out of hand. A young boy who did not want to move on because he was so ashamed of his scars was easy to deal with. Less easy was an elderly man who was very upset about his beard being singed and had died of shock. He was very proud of his beard and felt he could not possibly cross over if it was imperfect! However, once I had shown him how he could get a new, younger body with a beard that was black rather than grey, he was absolutely delighted and promptly called for his deceased wife to come for him.

When I met Pat, he was pretending to be a scarecrow! His father had cleared off when he was a baby, his mother had found that the only way she could keep the two of them was by prostitution, and he had spent his entire life on the margins of society. When I talked to Pat about his current status, he commented,

'Alive or dead, makes no difference!' He had never managed to find a niche and, since he regarded birds as his only friends, he was ironically acting as a scarecrow so that 'they at least would take notice of me'. We then found out that he had had a long series of lives in which he had felt 'worthless' and I told him that the time had now come for him to break the cycle. When I explained that in order to do this he would first have to cross over, the only helpers he could think of were a group of swallows (who instantly obliged).

Libby was Pat's mother and also felt that she had always been on the scrapheap. She was vaguely aware of being dead, but did not know where to go. Her life of prostitution had caused her to hate men, but there was one man (Denis, not Pat's father) whom she said she had really loved. Denis had died in Libby's arms a long time before she had, and was very happy to be called for.

In spite of all Gandhi's wonderful work, not to mention the equality always preached by Sathya Sai Baba and other Masters, misuse of the caste system in India unfortunately still persists. A Harijan whom I encountered on one of my journeys had not progressed because he felt himself to be an outcast even on the other side. I had to convince him that caste did not really exist, and then he called for his father.

Remaining in India for a moment, the audience of Anil, the above-mentioned 'guru' who was overly self-important, had been brainwashed into feeling themselves unworthy of Heaven. Fortunately, however, they only needed a little encouragement to think of a relative to call for.

A very different case was that of Clive, who had never been appreciated for himself, but was nevertheless quite a good pianist. So after he had died he just kept on and on playing the piano because it was the only way he had ever found to please people. Once we had talked a bit about his problem, and he had accepted my assurance that he did have other qualities besides his musicianship, he called for the aunt who was the only person who had ever shown him any affection.

On another occasion – to my great surprise – I saw a worm, but it turned out not to be a worm, but a man called Nathaniel, who had been brought up (particularly by the Church!) to think of himself as a lowly worm. I managed to get him to shed the worm's body and he was then revealed as a rather insignificant-looking man and all scrunched up. Once, however, I had got him to see the divine light inside himself, his appearance was completely transformed, and he was then able to call for his grandfather.

As I mentioned before, I have found several times that being stuck in the astral realms is not uniquely confined to human souls. On one occasion I met a snake, who told me that snakes were cursed and condemned to crawl on their bellies for ever. This grieved him because he wanted to be a bird, so I told him about evolution. Then a couple of birds kindly flew down and carried him away.

13. Suicide

Although it is often understandable, suicide is rarely, if ever, a solution to a problem. Especially since karma dictates that funking the Life Plan which we agreed to before coming in will necessitate our going through the same difficulties – probably augmented – in a future lifetime. The norm seems to be for people who take their own life to find themselves lost in a sort of Limbo after leaving their body. Certainly this was true of Christine, a woman I had known many years previously in Cottingham, East Yorkshire (where we lived before moving to Ludlow). She was still in a shadowy place, and in something akin to the state of mind that had driven her to take such a drastic measure.

In contrast to Christine, however, I met the husband of a good friend of mine – I'll call him 'Derek' – whose state of depression had caused him to kill himself. He told me that, largely thanks to my friend's prayers, he had now emerged from the 'shadowy place' and was working to help other people who had committed suicide. Since they had lived not far from each other, he was vaguely aware of Christine's fate, and when I talked to her about Derek and his work, she proved willing to accept his help and let him lead her across to the other side.

Eddie could also have come into the 'Guilt' section, but I am mentioning him here because it was guilt that had sadly driven him to suicide. Ludlow has had a May fair for centuries, and Eddie was responsible for the merry-go-round – I would guess a couple of hundred years ago. One year during his career there was an accident in which several children were killed and he was consumed with guilt because he knew that he should have checked the equipment better beforehand. I persuaded him that there was little point in going on feeling guilty for centuries, that the children had probably all returned to Earth by now, and that it was high time to forgive himself. He then called for Geoff, his boss, and apologized to him before allowing himself to be led to the other side.

Jonathan had lived in a hamlet in our area that no longer exists. (I got the impression that it may have been replaced by the Ludlow Business Park.) He found it very hard to make a living, and had hanged himself when he found that his second wife was messing around with other men. Marie, his first wife, had really loved him, however, and so was only too happy to lead him away from the 'grey place' in which he had been stuck for quite a long time.

Jean-Marc in Paris had thrown himself under a train and was furious to find that he was still 'alive'! He had previously made several vain attempts at suicide, which included slashing his wrists and, since he did not believe in the afterlife, had decided to do something that he thought would be foolproof. He was right about that of course, and so was able to accept my comment that he had now proved that he had an immortal soul. He had had a difficult life ever since the death of his mother when he was a child, and so, once convinced that he really had left his body and needed to cross over, he called for his mother to collect him.

Another Parisian suicide was a man called Luc, who had worked as a 'bouqinste' (bookseller) at the edge of the River Seine. He had battled with depression for many years and then finally thrown himself into the Seine. (He must have done it at

night, when there was nobody around to save him.) His wife had died before him, so I was able to get him to call for her.

Lucy was a teenage girl whose adoptive mother had caused her to kill herself by continually trying to make the poor child be like her. Lucy also knew that her birth mother had rejected her, and she had never come to terms with that. Fortunately she had had a loving grandmother so, once I had assured her that the grandmother had also died by now, she was willing to call upon her for help.

Our visit to Peru was one of the greatest experiences of my life, but I did not fall in love with Lima. One of its worst features is the *garúa,* a horrible grey mist that envelops the city for a good (or maybe I should say 'bad'!) proportion of the year. We were not spared this during our short stay there, and our guide told us that it was wont to cause depression – and on occasion even suicide – among the capital's inhabitants. On a journey that I did the following month I encountered Andrés, who had killed himself in Lima under the illusion that this would enable him to escape the *garúa.* He was glad to be assured that there was in fact an escape, and his mother came happily as soon as she was called.

Another Peruvian depressive was Juan, who had jumped into the Colca Canyón (which is even deeper than the Grand Canyon). Since he had already learned that this was not the way to cure his depression, he was very ready to call for his mother.

In January 2012 I met two of the people who had burned themselves in protest about Tibet. I told them that it was a useless way of handling the situation and that if they crossed over they would be in a much better position to help the people of Tibet. Then another of those who had committed suicide in this way appeared, saying that he had realized the error of his ways and could help them. He took the more stubborn of the two, and the other one called for a relative.

I have yet to meet a suicide bomber, but maybe one of you readers will do so. If so, I should love to hear about it, please!

14. Being in Hell

As I said earlier, Hell does indeed exist, but we make it for ourselves while still on Earth and then simply carry it on when we have died. That is, until we are rescued. This, however, is not one of the easiest of tasks and so far I have not on my journeying been taken to the Hell realms very often. Maybe I still need more practice in that domain, but I have nevertheless got a few examples.

Gladys, for instance, was an old woman who had had a

phobia of cats during her life and had drowned vast numbers of them. So now she was in her self-made Hell, in which she was being continually attacked by cats. So I explained to her that all she needed to do was apologize to the cats she had killed, and fortunately she did not find this too difficult. Then the cats who had been attacking her promptly all became friendly and gentle, Gladys became reconciled to them, and she called for her mother to come for her.

Frère Jean-Pierre was a very fat French monk who had been the cook in his monastery and had secretly always eaten more than his share. Now he was in his self-made Hell, being tantalized by dishes that were just out of his reach. When I asked him whether he had any interests other than food, he replied, 'Drink'! So I took him back to his childhood so that we could see that it was lack of love that had caused his over-indulgence. He then remembered that as a child he had a passion for cats, and so I asked him to think of one that had died which he had been particularly fond of. Since the Church had taught him that animals could not go to Heaven because they did not have souls, he was delighted when I told him to call for that much-loved cat to escort him over.

On another occasion I met four Satanists who were having a ceremony and wanted me to join in. I refused politely but firmly and then, together with my helpers, caused their thought-form Satan quickly to evaporate. This surprised and shocked the Satanists, but they still felt unable to cross over on account of being themselves 'completely black through and through'. I assured them that they still had a tiny light inside them and made them each find it. Once they had done so, I told them to focus on it and make it grow. When all four internal lights had grown sufficiently, each of the men was able to call for a deceased relative who had been important to him. I then saw that there were four shadowy figures standing in the wings, who had obviously been waiting for the men for a long time. So then there were some happy reunions and a speedy crossing.

A horrible Hell scene involved about 20 people who were performing some sort of Satanic ritual in which they were trying to catch the souls of small children as they left Earth and roast them to eat. I pointed out that they were not getting any satisfaction from this exercise and that helping people was much more satisfying. Then Apu, our beloved dog who had died not long beforehand, appeared. He transformed himself into a larger dog and saved one of the little ones by carrying him on his back to his mother. The 20 'Satanists' agreed that it was good to see the look of joy on the bereaved mother's face and were then persuaded to call for help to cross over themselves.

On another occasion I met a frog! It turned out to be a girl called Sharon, who believed herself to be a princess but who had

been turned into a frog as punishment for seducing large numbers of men. Her parents had treated her badly and she had grown up to despise men. It was of course a relief to her to find out that she did not need to remain a frog and, after we had talked about her upbringing and the fact that she deserved better, she was able to call for her grandmother, of whom she had a few good memories.

The 'Hell fire' preached in his church was so real for Desmond that he had, when he died, found himself 'deservedly burning in Hell'. I began by putting out the flames with a hosepipe and then showed him that his etheric body was indestructible. Then I told him that I did not want to know anything about the 'terrible crime' he had committed and that the only important thing was to forgive himself. That was clearly a bit difficult for Desmond, but he was nevertheless able to enlist the help of his father.

Jim was also making his own Hell after having been caught stealing a bit of cash from Bristol Cathedral. I found him at the gallows on the green outside the cathedral, surrounded by a large crowd of accusatory people. I discovered that he had been orphaned and alone nearly all his life and had been near starvation when his crime was committed. His feeling of guilt was great because he believed it to be worse to steal from a church than from someone wealthy. He was incredulous when I told him that he could escape from the unpleasant crowd, but then relieved when I said that all he needed to do was apologize to one of the cathedral clerics. He mentioned a Reverend Donald and was delighted when I told him that, since this cleric was now dead too, he could call for him, give his apology, and then be taken off to a better place.

Miranda's Hell was rather unusual. Having been herself scared as a child, she was now 'enjoying' scaring other children by pretending to be a sort of Medusa. Once I had convinced her that she was not really enjoying it, she removed the snakes from her hair and changed back into the beautiful black-haired woman she had been a long time ago. She had never been given any love, but she had had a remote figure of a grandfather whom she had admired, so she called for him.

Sandy, on the other hand, was filled with remorse about having killed her uncle, who had tried to rape her. Her Hell was feeling responsible for 'filling the River Teme with blood' and, despite the uncle having provoked her crime, she believed herself to be stuck there 'for ever'. Once I had convinced her that she was not to blame – or at least not entirely – she called for her father.

I wonder how long it will take the Churches to realize that Hell is of human making rather than God's. Or will they simply need to cease to exist before we can all become enlightened?

V

Conclusion

And finally lead us, great or small,
To that mighty banquet hall,
Where food and drink in every measure
Fill our hungry souls at leisure,
And breaking bread and drinking wine
Makes kindly fellowship divine.
The gods look down; their work is done.
Now Nature, Spirit, Soul are one!
From Dr. Roger Woolger's 'Invocation', written at a conference
in Dunderry, Ireland, June 2008

I could never be a novelist, and so one of the reasons I believe in the things that I encounter on my shamanic journeying is that I know I could never have made up stories such as those I have just recounted. Especially the ones that seem the most far fetched! In Deep Memory Process therapy, we are taught to point out to incredulous clients that what they have seen (or heard or felt) 'must have come from *somewhere*', and so I now extend this to my own journeying to convince my often skeptical mind.

Although I divided my case histories into 14 categories, a few of them do not fit exactly into any of these. One interesting example is Clarence and Algernon, who were in a cemetery in Shrewsbury fighting over (of all things!) a burial plot. They both wanted the plot that was situated closest to the chapel because they thought that it would be the fastest route to Heaven. I succeeded in convincing them that they no longer needed to select their plot since the one they were fighting over already had a gravestone on it and was therefore obviously occupied already. The name engraved on it turned out to be Algernon's but, after convincing them that they were both dead, I assured Clarence that he would be able to cross over just as fast as Algernon could and so they might as well make friends now. They saw the point and each called for a grandfather.

Another one was Doris, who had worked as a maid for a Mr. and Mrs. Hamilton in Canterbury in south-eastern England. Canterbury, like Ludlow, has a large number of historic buildings, and the Hamiltons' house is now a popular café. Doris was always extremely hard-working, but the Hamiltons were rather ruthless employers and, when the poor girl was stricken with TB (or consumption as it was called in her day), they scolded her constantly for slacking. In the end she was taken off to a sanatorium (or the equivalent of the time), where she died, but her desire to prove to her employers that she was ill rather than lazy had kept Doris Earthbound. I showed her how time had moved on, what had happened to the house, and assured her that Mr. and Mrs. Hamilton were now long dead too. This meant that in order to confront them with the truth, Doris would have to cross over, so she called for her mother to show her the way.

Yet another rather strange, and unclassifiable, case was that of an Englishman named Rupert, who was stuck in Africa. He had killed large numbers of Africans because he did not believe that they were 'real people'. (One could of course label him as ignorant, but his ignorance was not about the afterlife like my 'category 2' cases.) When I told him that we white people were in fact in the minority in the world, he was not at all happy, so then I told him that, if he wanted, he could go to an 'English Heaven'. I said this simply because he clearly had a great deal to learn and I thought he could do that more easily on the other side. Once assured that he would not have to continue to be surrounded by 'savages', he was happy to call for his father.

Rupert, like several other cases I have mentioned, is an example of someone who clearly has a lot of learning to do, but I am not making any suggestion that in this work we need to take full responsibility for that. Often one sees that the souls one is trying to help will be able to continue their necessary learning once they have crossed over, and there are of course many able teachers on the other side who are always willing and able to take over from us. The first, and most important step, is simply to persuade them that they will do much better by leaving the Earth's plane, and so showing how to do that has been the aim of this book.

However, I believe this work to be valuable also for those who practice it while still incarnate. All the great spiritual teachers say that we die according to how we have lived, and here I should like to recommend yet again Sogyal Rinpoche's classic, *The Tibetan Book of Living and Dying*.[1] Coming across a soul who is, for instance, completely trapped in anger can be a good reminder of just how harmful such emotions can be, and this can surely encourage us to work constantly on our own negative traits.

Finally, there is another thing that we can do in advance to help ourselves with our own death. On Simon Buxton's 'Death, Dying and the Beyond' workshop, he got us to practice dying, and I personally found this to be a wonderful experience. Following a great deal of reading on near-death experiences (commonly known as NDEs), I, who had always been terrified of such things as roller coasters, did not at all fancy the notion of being whooshed through a tunnel even though I knew that one could expect to come out from it into a beautiful light. My guides clearly appreciated my feelings here because, when I did this exercise at the workshop, I found myself being invited to step on to a beautiful boat, decorated in Indian style. The boat already had two occupants, both of whom I felt I knew from old, and once on it, I was rowed gently away across a beautiful lake. When I have remembered to repeat this exercise at home on my own, my experience has always been similar. I find it extremely comforting and fully intend to practice it more often once I feel that 'my time' is coming nearer.

So, in conclusion, I hope that this little book will have inspired you both to help those who are stuck on the Earth's plane and to take steps to ensure that your own inevitable departure will not be unnecessarily delayed.

Notes

Part I Introduction

1. Michael Harner, *The Way of the Shaman*, HarperSanFrancisco.
2. Jeremy Naydler, *Shamanic Wisdom in the Pyramid Texts: The Mystical Tradition of Ancient Egypt*, Inner Traditions, Vermont, 2005.
3. Robert Levy and Dr. Eve Bruce, *Shamanism: The Book of Journeys*, O-Books, 2010.
4. Dr. Eve Bruce, *Shaman, MD: A Plastic Surgeon's Remarkable Journey into the World of Shape Shifting*, Destiny Books, Vermont, 2002.
5. The Director of The Sacred Trust is Simon Buxton, and his book *The Shamanic Way of the Bee* (Destiny Books, Vermont, 2004) is absolutely fascinating.
6. For further information on Alberto Villoldo's training and books, see www.fourwinds.com.

Part II How This Book Came About

1. Ann Merivale, *Karmic Release: Journeying back to the Self*, Sai Towers Publishing, Bangalore, 2006.
2. Ann Merivale, *Souls United: The Power of Divine Connection*, Llewellyn, USA, 2009.
3. I again strongly recommend Simon Buxton's *The Shamanic Way of the Bee: Ancient Wisdom and the Healing Practices of the Bee Masters*, Destiny Books, Vermont, 2004.
4. Peter Richelieu, *A Soul's Journey*, Thorsons (HarperCollins), London, 1996.
5. Dr. Michael Newton, *Destiny of Souls*, Llewellyn Worldwide, USA, 2002.
6. Ann Merivale, *Discovering the Life Plan: Eleven Steps to Your Destiny*, O-Books, 2012.
7. Joan Grant, *Winged Pharaoh*, Ariel Press, USA, 1985.

8. William Baldwin, *Regression Therapy: Spirit Releasement*, 1992.

9. Wilma Davidson, *Spirit Rescue: A Simple Guide to Talking with Ghosts and Freeing Earthbound Spirits*, Llewellyn, USA, 2007.

Part III The Procedure

1. Richard Webster, *Spirit Guides and Angel Guardians: Contact Your Invisible Helpers*, Llewellyn, USA, 1999.

2. See Ann Merivale, *Karmic Release: Journeying back to the Self*, Sai Towers Publishing, Bangalore, 2006.

3. See Philippa Merivale, *Rescued by Angels*, O-Books, London and Washington, 2009.

4. Ann Merivale, *Souls United: The Power of Divine Connection*, Llewellyn, USA, 2009.

5. Ann Merivale, *Discovering the Life Plan: Eleven Steps to Your Destiny*, O-Books, 2012.

6. For information on Sathya Sai Baba, see Chapter 2 of my book *Souls United*.

7. www.sacredtrust.org.

8. Malidoma Patrice Somé, *Of Water and the Spirit: Ritual, Magic and Initiation in the Life of an African Shaman*, Compass (Penguin), USA, 1994.

Part IV The Reasons Why Souls Get Stuck on the Earth's Plane

1. Ann Merivale, *Souls United: The Power of Divine Connection*, Llewellyn, USA, 2009.

2. 1 John 4:18, King James Version.

3. Neil Forsyth, *Delete This at Your Peril*.

4. Malidoma Patrice Somé, *Of Water and the Spirit: Ritual, Magic and Initiation in the Life of an African Shaman*, Compass (Penguin), USA, 1994.

Part V Conclusion

1. Sogyal Rinpoche, *The Tibetan Book of Living and Dying*.

BOOKS

6th Books investigates the paranormal, supernatural, explainable or unexplainable. Titles cover everything included within parapsychology: how to, lifestyles, beliefs, myths, theories and memoir.